Coordinator and Instructor Guide for Basic Trauma Life Support for Paramedics and Other Advanced Providers

Fifth Edition

Coordinator and Instructor Guide for Basic Trauma Life Support for Paramedics and Other Advanced Providers

Fifth Edition

John Emory Campbell, MD, FACEP
Alabama Chapter
American College of Emergency Physicians

PEARSON

Prentice Hall

Upper Saddle River, New Jersey 07458

Publisher: Julie Levin Alexander
Publisher's Assistant: Regina Bruno
Senior Acquisitions Editor: Tiffany Price Salter
Editorial Assistant: Joanna Rodzen-Hickey
Senior Marketing Manager: Katrin Beacom
Channel Marketing Manager: Rachele Strober
Marketing Coordinator: Janet Ryerson
Director of Production and Manufacturing: Bruce Johnson
Managing Editor for Production: Patrick Walsh

Production Liaison: Julie Li
Production Editor: Bruce Hobart/Pine Tree Composition, Inc.
Manufacturing Manager: Ilene Sanford
Manufacturing Buyer: Pat Brown
Creative Director: Cheryl Asherman
Composition: Pine Tree Composition, Inc.
Printing and Binding: The Banta Company
Cover Printer: Phoenix Color Corp.

Pearson Education, Ltd., *London*
Pearson Education Australia Pty. Limited, *Sydney*
Pearson Education Singapore, Pte. Ltd.
Pearson Education North Asia Ltd., *Hong Kong*
Pearson Education Canada, Ltd., *Toronto*

Pearson Educaçion de Mexico, S.A. de C.V.
Pearson Education—Japan, *Tokyo*
Pearson Education Malaysia, Pte. Ltd.
Pearson Education, Upper Saddle River, *New Jersey*

Notice: The authors and the publisher of this volume have taken care that the information and technical recommendations contained herein are based on research and expert consultation, and are accurate and compatible with the standards generally accepted at the time of publication. Nevertheless, as new information becomes available, changes in clinical and technical practices becomes necessary. The reader is advised to carefully consult manufacturers' instructions and information material for all supplies and equipment before use, and to consult with a healthcare professional as necessary. This advice is espcially important when using new supplies or equipment for clinical purposes. The authors and publisher disclaim all responsibility for any liability, loss, injury, or damage incurred as a consequence, directly or indirectly, of the use and application of any of the contents of this volume.

10 9 8 7 6 5 4 3 2 1
ISBN 0-13-112353-X

Contents

Mission Statement
of the BTLS Organization

Basic Trauma Life Support International, Inc. is a global organization dedicated to decreasing death and disability from trauma by education and emergency trauma care.

Preface

The Alabama Chapter of the American College of Emergency Physicians (ACEP) developed the Basic Trauma Life Support (BTLS) course in 1982. The decision to develop such a course was based on the need for good "hands-on" continuing education courses for EMTs and other EMS personnel. BTLS has since become accepted internationally as the standard training course for prehospital trauma care, and now is not only taught as a continuing education course but also used in many EMT training programs. BTLS courses are monitored and certified by their local BTLS chapter. This instructor and coordinator guide is designed to help you conduct an organized BTLS course. Student texts and slides are available to be used with this manual. The BTLS course is usually conducted over a two-day period, but if time is available, this material can be better taught over a longer period, such as during EMT training. Information about how to schedule a certified course in your area can be obtained by contacting the BTLS International office:

Basic Trauma Life Support International, Inc.
1 S. 280 Summit Avenue, Court B
Oakbrook Terrace, IL 60181
Phone U.S.: 1-800-495-BTLS
Phone outside U.S.: 1-630-495-6442
Fax: 630-495-6404
E-mail: info@btls.org
Internet: http://www.btls.org

Coordinator and Instructor Guide for Basic Trauma Life Support for Paramedics and Other Advanced Providers

Fifth Edition

1

Overview of the Basic and Advanced Courses

Trauma is the leading cause of death for Americans under age 40. During the course of a year, almost 1 in every 4 Americans is injured and 1 in 20 is disabled to some degree. The majority of seriously injured patients arrive at small emergency departments, where a nurse has to care for them until a physician can be called. For these patients the difference between recovery and death is often measured in minutes. Thus, the care provided by these rescuers is crucial.

The basic course is designed to teach EMT-Bs and first responders and the advanced course is designed to teach paramedics, advanced EMTs, and other advanced EMS providers the skills necessary to recognize mechanisms of injury, assess, perform critical interventions, package, and transport the trauma patient. The primary purpose of the course is to provide the student with the fundamental knowledge and experience necessary to get the trauma patient to the emergency department in the best possible condition so that the medical personnel there have the opportunity to use their advanced capabilities to save lives. A major focus of the course is the identification of conditions that require immediate transport ("load-and-go" conditions) in order to save the patient. Lifesaving techniques are taught or reviewed in practical exercises. Where possible, newly developed equipment is provided so the students may become familiar with state-of-the-art techniques and equipment.

While the course is designed for the prehospital phase of EMS, it is also useful to medical students, first-year emergency medicine residents, registered nurses, nurse practitioners, and physician assistants interested in trauma care. Not only will the lectures and most of the skills be useful to them; they also will get a unique view of the world in which EMTs must function. It is very different form the "cozy confines" of the emergency department.

COURSE SYNOPSIS

The two-day format for BTLS courses is considered the most practical, even though it limits lecture time and requires precise timing of practice stations. Most students and faculty simply do not have more than two days available to attend courses. Where there are no time constraints, you may take more time with both the lectures and skill stations and thus enhance learning the material. An excellent way to do this is to teach the course over 2½ days, in the evenings twice a week, or over a college semester. Sample schedules will be given.

LECTURES

Coordination of the lectures is of utmost importance. The lectures set the stage for the weekend, and equipment malfunction or speaker delays detract from the remainder of the course. The lecture assignments may be divided among the instructors or handled by one instructor as desired. The course director and coordinator should take into consideration the person's ability to lecture. It is important that the instructors are assigned and have the slides and/or slide guide two weeks before the course. It is advisable that each instructor be given the questions pertaining to his or her lecture that will appear on the written examination. It is also important for the course director to be available in the event that an instructor is late or does not show. The coordinator or course director must get the lecturers started and finished on time. Slides should be collected immediately after the presentation. The BTLS course for basic providers has one less lecture (The Trauma Cardiopulmonary Arrest) than the course for advanced providers.

SKILL STATION ROTATIONS (BTLS FOR ADVANCED PROVIDERS)

The students must be assigned to groups for skill station rotations. The best way to do this is to divide them into seven groups (the number of skill stations; see the following tentative schedules) and assign a number for each group for the skill station rotations. It does not matter if all of the groups do not have the same number of students.

> **EXAMPLE**: If there were 24 students, you would have four groups of three students and three groups of four students. You can't do this ahead of time because some students don't show up. With the students still seated, point out "1, 2, 3, Group One. 1, 2, 3, Group Two," and so on. Tell them to report to the skill station that is the same as their group number. In other words, Group One goes to Station 1, Group Two to Station 2, and so on. Explain to the students that when the timekeeper announces "CHANGE STATIONS," each group will rotate up one number. For example, Group One goes to Station 2, Group Two goes to Station 3, and so on. Also explain that when rotating from Station 7, that group goes to Station 1. See tentative schedules that follow.

SKILL STATION ROTATIONS (BTLS FOR BASIC PROVIDERS)

There is one less skill station (Chest Decompression/IV/IO) for basic providers. Some courses mingle the students and simply have the basic providers go through all of the skill stations with the advanced providers (getting a break during the advanced portion of the skill stations). If you are doing it this way, then use the aforementioned method to divide the students. If you are only training basic providers, use the following method.

The students must be assigned to groups for skill station rotations. The best way to do this is to divide them into six groups (the number of skill stations; see the following tentative schedules) and assign a number for each group for the skill station rotations. It does not matter if all of the groups do not have the same number of students.

> **EXAMPLE**: If there were 20 students, you would have four groups of three students and two groups of four students. You can't do this ahead of time because some students don't show up. With the students still seated, point out "1, 2, 3, Group One. 1, 2, 3, Group Two," and so on. Tell them to report to the skill station that is the same as their group number. In other words, Group One goes to Station 1, Group Two to Station 2, and so on. Explain to the students that when the timekeeper announces "CHANGE STATIONS," each group will rotate up one number. For exam-

ple, Group One goes to Station 2, Group Two goes to Station 3, and so on. Also explain that when rotating from Station 7, that group goes to Station 1. See tentative schedules that follow.

PATIENT ASSESSMENT SCENARIO PRACTICE AND TESTING

The scenario assessment stations are the heart of the course. They integrate the student's professional experience, the lectures, and the skill stations. They are the stage for the hands-on learning of basic trauma life support. You may choose from the patient assessment scenarios in Chapter 4, or you may make up your own scenarios. If you make up your own scenarios, please send BTLS International, Inc. copies, as we may want to include them in the next *Coordinator and Instructor Guide.* Because the Glasgow Coma Score (GCS) is now used in patient assessment, you must provide a copy of the GCS for the students to use when they practice and test (they are not expected to memorize it). You can copy the GSC on page 219 of the *Coordinator and Instructor Guide.*

The number of scenarios that you use will depend on the number of students who are taking the course. You need one scenario station for each three students. You will never have less than six scenario stations as you need that many for a group of three (three practices, three tests). You will almost always need an extra scenario station for retests, but this can be put together at the end of the day if you are short of instructors. You need two instructors for each patient assessment station, one to interact with the students and one to fill out the gradesheet. If you mingle basic and advanced students, the only change that you must make is to have both advanced and basic gradesheets in the teaching and testing scenarios. The instructor will use the gradesheet corresponding to the training of the student practicing or being tested.

When your students are ready to be assigned for rotation of their practice and testing scenarios, they need to be divided into groups of three (3).

EXAMPLE: If there are 24 students, you would have eight groups of three students. With the students still seated, point out "1, 2, 3, Group One. 1, 2, 3, Group Two", and so on. Tell them to report to the patient assessment station that is the same as their group number. In other words, Group One goes to Station 1, Group Two to Station 2, and so on. Explain to the students that when the timekeeper announces "CHANGE STATIONS," each group will rotate up one number. For example, Group One goes to Station 2, Group Two goes to Station 3, and so on. Also explain that when rotating from the last station, that group goes to Station 1.

If your head count leaves you with two students in the last group, they can rotate as a group of two. If your head count leaves you with one student in the last group, take that student and one student from the last group and make two groups of two. A group of four students will not allow your stations to rotate smoothly.

Each scenario station should have three rotations for practice at 20 minutes per rotation, and three rotations for testing at 10 minutes per rotation. These times may vary according to your discretion.

The groups of two students will rotate to the third practice station. One of the students will practice twice. This makes it fair that they are able to practice three times the same as everyone else. When they move to the fourth station, it will be a test like everyone else. However, after both students test, they will be finished.

By using this system, your rotations will be smooth with very little coordinating, and nothing needs to be written down. Students who do not show up for the course will not affect your rotations. Enough copies of gradesheets must be made so that each station will have enough for all the teams that practice and test. A gradesheet is filled out for each team (specifically, the team leader) that practices or tests in a station.

EXAMPLES OF COURSE TIMETABLES

The classic BTLS course schedule has had lectures in the morning and skills in the afternoon both days. It was originally done this way to follow the example of the ATLS and ACLS courses. The schedule was designed to give the students a break after four hours of lectures. The problem with this is that you are teaching skills that will not be covered in a lecture until the second day. The Texas chapter of BTLS has modified the schedule so that all of the lectures are taught the first day, all of the skill stations are taught the second morning, and the second afternoon is spent in testing. Many of the students find this more acceptable in spite of facing eight hours of lectures on the first day. This schedule also allows you to have fewer instructors the first day. BTLS International has taken no stand on this issue, and you may choose whichever works best for you. Samples of both schedules are provided.

SAMPLE COURSE TIMETABLES (ADVANCED PROVIDERS)

Sample Course Timetable (advanced): Two-Day Course, Lectures Both Days

First day

Sign-In and Collection of Pretests	30 min
Welcome and Introduction	5 min
Blood and Body Fluid Precautions	10 min
Scene Size-Up	30 min
Assessment and Initial Management	45 min
Patient Assessment Demonstration	15 min
Break	15 min
Airway Management	30 min
Shock Evaluation and Management	30 min
Lunch and Faculty Meeting	60 min
Chest and Abdominal Trauma	30 min
Head and Spinal Trauma	30 min
Extremity Trauma	30 min

Skill Stations (30 minutes each)

1. Basic and Advanced Airway
2. Short Backboard/KED/Rapid Extrication
3. Traction Splint/Splinting
4. Patient Assessment
5. Chest Decompression/IV/IO
6. Helmet/Log-Roll/Long Backboard
7. Patient Assessment

Faculty Meeting	30 min

Second Day

Burns	45 min
Trauma in Pregnancy	30 min
Trauma in Children	45 min
Break	15 min
Trauma in the Elderly	25 min
Patients under the Influence	20 min
Patient Assessment Scenarios	60 min
Lunch and Faculty meeting	60 min
Patient Assessment Scenarios	90 min
Practical and Written Examination	120 min
Faculty Meeting	30 min
Results to Students	

Sample Course Timetable (advanced): Two-Day Course, Lectures First Day

First Day

Sign-In and Collection of Pretests	30 min
Welcome and Introduction	15 min
Scene Size-Up	30 min
Patient Assessment, Trauma Arrest, and Patient Assessment Demonstration	60 min
Break	15 min
Trauma in Pregnancy/Elderly Trauma	45 min
Shock	30 min
Trauma in Children	45 min
Lunch	60 min
Chest Trauma	30 min
Head Trauma	30 min
Airway Management	30 min
Abdominal/Extremity Trauma	45 min
Break	15 min
Burns	45 min
Spinal Trauma	30 min
Blood and Body Substance Precautions	10 min
Patient Assessment Demonstration	15 min
Faculty Meeting	30 min

Second Day

Patient Assessment Demo, Questions and Answers	30 min

Skill Stations (30 minutes each)

1. Basic and Advanced Airway
2. Short Backboard/KED/Rapid Extrication
3. Traction Splint/Splinting
4. Patient Assessment
5. Chest Decompression/IV/IO
6. Helmet/Log-Roll/Long Backboard
7. Patient Assessment

Lunch	60 min
Written Test	30 min
Practice and Testing Scenario Stations	120 min
Faculty Meeting	30 min
Results to Students	

Sample Course Timetable (advanced): Two-and-a-Half-Day Course

First Evening

Faculty Meeting	15 min
Sign-In and Collection of Pretests	30 min
Welcome and Introduction	15 min
Scene Size-Up	30 min
Patient Assessment, Trauma Arrest	
Patient Assessment Demonstration	60 min
Break	15 min
Patient Assessment Practice	90 min

The students should be divided into groups of 6. There should be enough stations set up (4 for a class of 24 or 6 for a class of 36) for each group to watch one patient assessment demonstration and then divide into two groups of three to practice patient assessment.

Second Day

Sign-In and Coffee	30 min
Airway Management	30 min
Chest Trauma/Shock	60 min
Spinal Cord Trauma	30 min
Break	15 min
Head Trauma	30 min

Abdominal/Extremity Trauma	45 min
Burns	30 min
Lunch and Faculty meeting	60 min

Skill Stations (30 minutes each)

1. Basic and Advanced Airway
2. Short Backboard/KED/Rapid Extrication
3. Traction Splint/Splinting
4. Chest Decompression/IV/IO
5. Helmet/Log-Roll/Long Backboard

Faculty Meeting	30 min

Third Day

Sign-In and Coffee	30 min
Trauma in Pregnancy/Elderly Trauma	30 min
Trauma in Children	30 min
Patients under the Influence	15 min
Blood and Body Fluid Precautions	15 min
Break and Faculty Meeting	15 min
Patient Assessment Practice and Testing	90 min
Lunch	60 min
Written Test	30 min
Continue Patient Assessment Practice and Testing	
Faculty Meeting	30 min
Results to the Students	

SAMPLE COURSE TIMETABLES (BASIC PROVIDERS)

Sample Course Timetable (Basic): Two-Day Course, Lectures Both Days

First Day

Sign-In and Collection of Pretests	30 min
Welcome and Introduction	5 min
Blood and Body Fluid Precautions	10 min
Scene Size-Up	30 min
Assessment and Initial Management	45 min
Patient Assessment Demonstration	15 min
Break	15 min
Airway Management	30 min
Shock Evaluation and Management	30 min

Lunch and Faculty Meeting	60 min
Chest and Abdominal Trauma	30 min
Head and Spinal Trauma	30 min
Extremity Trauma	30 min

Skill Stations (30 minutes each)

1. Basic Airway
2. Short Backboard/KED/Rapid Extrication
3. Traction Splint/Splinting
4. Patient Assessment
5. Helmet/Log-Roll/Long Backboard
6. Patient Assessment

Faculty Meeting	30 min

Second Day

Burns	45 min
Trauma in Pregnancy	30 min
Trauma in Children	45 min
Break	15 min
Trauma in the Elderly	25 min
Patients under the Influence	20 min
Patient Assessment Scenarios	60 min
Lunch and Faculty Meeting	60 min
Patient Assessment Scenarios	90 min
Practical and Written Examination	120 min
Faculty Meeting	30 min
Results to Students	

Sample Course Timetable (Basic): Two-day Course, Lectures First Day

First Day

Sign-In and Collection of Pretests	30 min
Welcome and Introduction	15 min
Scene Size-Up	30 min
Patient Assessment and Patient Assessment Demonstration	60 min
Break	15 min
Trauma in Pregnancy/Elderly Trauma	45 min

Shock	30 min
Trauma in Children	45 min
Lunch	60 min
Head Trauma	30 min
Airway Management	30 min
Abdominal/Extremity Trauma	45 min
Break	15 min
Burns	45 min
Spinal Trauma	30 min
Patient Assessment Demonstration	15 min
Faculty Meeting	30 min

Second Day

Patient Assessment Demo, Questions and Answers	30 min

Skill Stations (30 minutes each)

1. Basic Airway
2. Short Backboard/KED/Rapid Extrication
3. Traction Splint/Splinting
4. Patient Assessment
5. Helmet/Log-Roll/Long Backboard
6. Patient Assessment

Lunch	60 min
Written Test	30 min
Practice and Testing Scenario Stations	120 min
Faculty Meeting	30 min
Results to Students	

Sample Course Timetable (Basic): Two-and-a-Half-Day Course

First Evening

Faculty Meeting	15 min
Sign-In and Collection of Pretests	30 min
Welcome and Introduction	15 min
Scene Size-Up	30 min
Patient Assessment and Patient Assessment Demonstration	60 min

Break	15 min
Patient Assessment Practice	90 min

The students should be divided into groups of 6. There should be enough stations set up (4 for a class of 24 or 6 for a class of 36) for each group to watch one patient assessment demonstration and then divide into two groups of three to practice patient assessment.

Second Day

Sign-In and Coffee	30 min
Airway Management	30 min
Chest Trauma	30 min
Shock	30 min
Spinal Cord Trauma	30 min
Break	15 min
Head Trauma	30 min
Abdominal/Extremity Trauma	45 min
Burns	30 min
Lunch and Faculty Meeting	60 min

Skill Stations (30 minutes each)

1. Basic Airway
2. Short Backboard/KED/Rapid Extrication
3. Traction Splint/Splinting
4. Helmet/Log-Roll/Long Backboard

Faculty Meeting	30 min

Third Day

Sign-In and Coffee	30 min
Trauma in Pregnancy/Elderly Trauma	30 min
Trauma in Children	30 min
Patients under the Influence	15 min
Blood and Body Fluid Precautions	15 min
Break and Faculty Meeting	15 min
Patient Assessment Practice and Testing	90 min
Lunch	60 min
Written Test	30 min
Continue Patient Assessment Practice and Testing	
Faculty Meeting	30 min
Results to the Students	

FACULTY MEETINGS

Precourse

This meeting has traditionally taken place after dinner the night before the course but may just as well be done early in the morning during course registration. This meeting serves several important functions:

1. Orient the faculty to each other and to the site.
2. Orient the faculty to the particular student composition (EMT-Bs, first responders, EMT-intermediates, paramedics, registered nurses, medical students, medical residents, etc.).
3. Update the final changes in the agenda.
4. Update the latest BTLS innovations and directives from the affiliate faculty present.
5. Review the goals and objectives of a BTLS course (see Chapter 5).
6. Remind that the discussion of students that takes place in the faculty meetings is to be kept in the meetings.
7. Review both the *Guide for Instructors* and the *Student Guide* to ensure consistency among instructors for the entire course.
8. Review available equipment and its distribution.
9. Review any skill station revisions.
10. Identify last-minute no-shows and forgotten lecture slide sets.
11. Encourage faculty to have a meeting at lunch each day to discuss the afternoon's practical stations.

Before Skill Station Rotations

This should be a brief meeting to review teaching techniques and objectives of the skill stations. Specifically stress that skill stations are not for lectures but for demonstration and hands-on training. Also stress that each session must begin and end on time.

Before Assessment Scenario Practice and Testing

The most consistent student complaint in course critiques has been inconsistency among the faculty members teaching and testing assessment scenarios. This meeting should review the following sections in both the text and instructor's guide:

1. Ground rules for team practice and testing (pages 47–49 basic and advanced textbook).
2. Breakdown of performance criteria.
3. How to fill out the grading sheet (specifically notes to be taken relative to student performance and critical identifying data).
4. Pass/fail criteria.
5. Retest policy.
6. Emphasis of need to orient models to the scenarios.
7. Reminder that the purpose of the faculty is to help the student learn enough to pass. Every effort must be made to identify weaknesses and assist the student's correction of them.

Postcourse

This meeting is to determine each student's final grade. When grading is completed, the faculty should be encouraged to critique the course and offer constructive suggestions for future courses.

Each student's written test scores and patient assessment scores (both practice and test) should be collated with the student's picture (optional) and considered by the faculty. A certified course requires a written test score of at least 74 percent and a scenario assessment score of at least "adequate." To be considered for instructor, a student must score at least 86 percent on the written test and should score "excellent" on scenario assessment testing (BTLS chapters may choose to use other criteria). Students may be retested on the scenario assessment immediately or within six weeks in order to pass the course. Students who fail the written test should not be retested immediately but should study their weaknesses and retest within six weeks. A student may not be retested in order to increase a passing grade to instructor potential. If a student fails the scenario assessment station, the faculty may consider the student's practice grade to see if perhaps a marginal increase in grade is warranted. The same is true if the student is a possible instructor candidate. The scenario practice grade cannot be used to lower a passing grade. In other words, the faculty should consider practice scores only if they are considering raising the student's grade. Because scenario assessment is a somewhat subjective score, there are always some changes (and a lot of lively discussion) at the faculty meeting. Any students who fail, especially if they fail the retest, should have careful documentation of why they failed. Students should always be allowed to review their written tests and scenario assessment grade sheets after the faculty meeting. Thus be very careful in your documentation.

Faculty Critique

This is usually the last time that the faculty will be together. Now is the time to collect comments from the faculty about the course and teaching material. How can they be improved? BTLS International is always interested in ways to improve the text, slides, and instructor's guide. All comments and suggestions are appreciated and carefully considered for changes in future editions. The future development of BTLS is dependent on the continued constructive criticism by students and faculty.

2

Administrative Considerations

FREQUENTLY ASKED QUESTIONS

What Is The Mission of the BTLS Organization?

BTLS is a global organization dedicated to preventing death and disability from trauma through education and emergency trauma care.

What Are the Goals and Objectives of the Basic and Advanced BTLS Courses?

1. Teach basic hands-on trauma care.
2. Teach a target audience of advanced EMTs, paramedics, and registered nurses for the advanced course and a target audience of EMT-Bs and first responders for the basic course.
3. Maintain quality assurance so that the same basics are consistently taught chapter to chapter and yet allow for regional differences.
4. Keep the course current.
5. Keep the course short enough to be taught in a weekend.
6. Strive to make teaching and learning BTLS simple and practical.
7. Keep the course conservative and noncontroversial so that the principles taught reflect the current standard of care.

Who Can Teach the Course?

Certified BTLS courses must be taught by BTLS instructors. To be a BTLS instructor, one must attend a certified BTLS course, score at least 86 percent on the written exam, and score "excellent" on patient assessment (chapters may choose to use other criteria). You must then take an instructor course and be monitored or take an instructor preceptorship (this varies from chapter to chapter). Basic BTLS instructors can only teach basic BTLS courses. Advanced BTLS instructors can teach basic or advanced courses. Physicians who are board certified in emergency medicine, or are ATLS providers, or who actively participate and teach trauma care may take the instructor course or preceptorship without taking the full provider course.

In unusual circumstances a physician or other EMS provider (EMT, nurse, nurse practitioner, or physician assistant) who has not taken the instructor course may help teach a BTLS course. However, this may be done only with the permission of the chapter BTLS medical director or committee. These requirements are necessary to maintain the high quality of certified courses.

Who Can Take the Course?

The advanced course material requires the ability to start intravenous fluids and to use advanced airway management. Advanced airway management is defined as the use of a blind insertion airway Device, or endotracheal tube. This limits the full course to advanced EMTs, paramedics, medical students, medical residents, registered nurses, nurse practitioners, and physician assistants. The basic course is for EMS personnel who cannot perform advanced procedures (basic EMTs, first responders, and licensed practical nurses).

How Many Students Can You Teach in a Course?

The number of students is limited by the number of faculty available to teach them. Because so much of the teaching is almost one to one, large classes cannot be taught. Most classes range from 24 to 36 students; however, if enough instructors are available, as many as 50 students may be taught.

How Many Instructors Are Required to Teach a Course?

See Selecting Faculty in Precourse Planning, pages 18–19.

What Must Be Taught in a BTLS Course?

Advanced BTLS

LECTURES
The first 22 chapters are considered "core" material and should be covered in all courses. All chapters in the appendix are optional and should *not* be covered in a two-day or two-and-a-half-day course (there is too much material to cover). If you are teaching BTLS as part of the curriculum of an EMT course, it is reasonable to include the appendix chapters.

SKILL STATIONS
1. Basic and Advanced Airway Management
2. Short Backboard/KED/Emergency Rapid Extrication
3. Traction Splints
4. Patient Assessment
5. Helmet Management/Log-Roll/Long Backboard
6. Chest Decompression/External Jugular IV/IO
7. Patient Assessment

Skill stations 1–7 are core. You are not expected to teach all types of traction splints. Teach the traction splint in common use in your area. In skill station 5, it is recommended that you teach the anterior chest technique. Both external jugular vein cannulation and intraosseous infusion are core, but some chapters do not teach external jugular vein cannulation if the students are already skilled in the procedure.

All chapters in the appendix are optional but may be taught if time permits. The students must be notified in advance if any optional material is to be covered.

Basic BTLS

The first 19 chapters are considered core material and should be covered in all courses. All chapters in the appendix are optional and should *not* be covered in a two-day or two-and-a-half-day course (there is too much material to cover). If you are teaching BTLS as part of the curriculum of an EMT course, it is reasonable to include the appendix chapters.

SKILL STATIONS

1. Basic Airway Management
2. Short Backboard/KED/Emergency Rapid Extrication
3. Traction Splints
4. Patient Assessment
5. Helmet Management/Log-Roll/Long Backboard
6. Patient Assessment

Skill stations 1–7 are core except for skill station 5, which is only taught in the advanced course. You are not expected to teach all types of traction splints. Teach the traction splint in common use in your area. All chapters in the appendix are optional but may be taught if time permits. The students must be notified in advance if any optional material is to be covered.

What Constitutes Course Completion?

A student may become a BTLS provider by attending the lectures and skill stations and by passing the written and practical examinations. BTLS providers will receive a card and/or certificate from the sponsoring chapter confirming that they have satisfactorily completed the course. Certification is good for three years. Such certification does not guarantee future performance, nor is it a form of licensure of any kind. Students who fail either the written or the practical examination after retesting will be given a letter of attendance so they may receive continuing education credit.

Recertification may be obtained by repeating the provider course or by taking a recertification course. Instructors may remain certified by teaching at least one course per year. A special course for instructor recertification is available.

What Are Pass-Fail Criteria?

A student who attends the lectures and skill stations, scores at least 74 percent on the written test, and at least "adequate" on patient assessment will pass the course. Students who fail the patient assessment test will usually be retested immediately (time permitting) or given the opportunity to retest within six weeks. Students who fail only the written test will be given the opportunity to retest within six weeks. Students who pass the retest will pass the course. Students who fail the retest *may* be provided an opportunity to retake the course at no charge or for a reduced charge. Students who fail both the written and patient assessment tests will be asked to repeat the course. Students who score at least 86 percent on the written and "excellent" on patient assessment may be asked to take the instructor course or preceptorship. Pass-fail criteria for the patient assessment test include the following:

Inadequate Rating

1. Disorganized exams
2. Prolonged on-scene times in the setting of load-and-go situations

3. Critical actions missed (such as not stabilizing the neck)
4. Making fatal errors (such as poor cervical spine management)
5. Causes death of the patient

Adequate Rating

1. Reasonable organization of assessment exams
2. Accurate identification of load-and-go situations
3. Abbreviated on-scene times for load-and-go situations
4. Performs critical actions
5. Makes no fatal errors

Good Rating

1. Organized exams and solid overall performance
2. Interacts well with patient and team members
3. Performs all critical actions
4. Abbreviated on-scene times for load-and-go situations
5. Correctly performs or oversees performance of all critical interventions

Excellent Rating

1. Excellent exams
2. Excellent patient care
3. Interacts well with patient and team members
4. Directs the team well; displays leadership
5. Performs all critical actions
6. Demonstrates clear understanding of prehospital trauma assessment and management
7. Cooperative and supportive in the learning environment
8. Conveys attitude of interest and desire to help teach trauma assessment and management

What Is The Retest Policy?

Students who fail the patient assessment test will usually be retested immediately (time permitting) or given the opportunity to retest within six weeks. Students who fail the written test may not retake it immediately but will be given an opportunity to retake the test after having had time to review the test and study identified areas of weakness. The retake of the written test will be within six weeks. Students who pass the retest will pass the course. Should the student fail the retest, he or she *may* be provided an opportunity to retake the course at no charge or for a reduced charge. Students who fail both the written and patient assessment tests will be asked to repeat the course. Students may not retest in order to raise a passing grade.

What Does Certification Mean?

To be certified as a BTLS provider or instructor means that the individual has passed a BTLS course taught by BTLS instructors under the sponsorship of the BTLS International Organization. It does not certify future performance, nor does it confer licensure of any kind.

How Does a BTLS Provider or Instructor Maintain Certification?

BTLS providers may maintain their certification by taking a BTLS provider or recertification course every three years. BTLS instructors may maintain their instructor certification by teaching three BTLS courses every three years and attending an instructor update or recertification course every two to three years (depending on local chapter policy).

Where Do I Get the Pretest and Posttest?

Your BTLS chapter office will provide the pretest and posttest when a certified course is scheduled. This practice ensures that your students will receive the most current version of the tests. This also aids exam security.

PRECOURSE PLANNING

Scheduling a Certified BTLS Course

A certified course must be scheduled through the BTLS organization in your chapter. If you do not know how to contact this organization in your area, you may obtain information by calling or writing:

Ginny Kennedy Palys
Executive Director
BTLS International, Inc.
1 S. 280 Summit Avenue, Court B
Oakbrook, IL 60181
Phone 1-800-495-BTLS
Phone outside U.S.: 630-495-6442
Fax: 630-495-6404
Internet: http://www.btls.org
E-mail: info@btls.org

Basic trauma life support texts, instructor guides, and slide sets may be purchased at a discount through your chapter BTLS office. They are also available from BTLS International by calling the number listed above.

Selecting a Course Coordinator

The course coordinator is the key to a successful program. This position requires someone who is organized and motivated since there is a considerable amount of work involved over several months. See Chapter 8 for the qualifications of a course coordinator.

Teamwork and communication are the keys to a successful BTLS course. The course coordinator must have a smooth working relationship and open communications with the course director and affiliate faculty, for it is their teamwork that determines the successful outcome. Together they must select the site and faculty for the course. These selections are made on the basis of availability and the time frame in which they are working. Usually, three months are needed for the development of a course from beginning to end, with the last two weeks being the most intense.

Selecting a Medical Director

The course medical director, or at least one of two co-directors, must be a physician BTLS instructor. It is best if the course director is also a local physician. A local physician is better able to appropriately integrate the material into the local prehospital and emergency department systems. A BTLS instructor physician is best prepared to present the material effectively in the manner in which it was designed. The director must take overall responsibility for the quality of the course. Responsibilities include being involved in the planning, scheduling, and actual teaching of the course. He or she must also see that the schedule allows adequate time for lectures and skill stations, including ensuring that lecturers stay within the given time frame. If any instructor is not present at the allotted time, the director should be able to fill in. The medical director may delegate some or all of these responsibilities to the affiliate faculty. The course director will chair the faculty meeting at the end of the course. If questions arise concerning grading, the vote of the majority of the faculty will prevail. The director will vote only in the case of a tie.

Selecting Faculty

The faculty for a certified BTLS course must consist of a course director, course coordinator, and enough instructors to teach the number of students registered (one instructor or the course medical director must be affiliate faculty). The course director must be a physician BTLS instructor. A physician who is not already an instructor may co-direct a course with a physician BTLS instructor. It is advisable to have two physicians and two nurses present on the course faculty to provide a balanced presentation of the trauma team concept. You must have at least one affiliate faculty at a course.

The number of instructors needed depends on the number of students: the patient assessment testing is one on one and requires many instructors in order to keep the length of the course within reason. The number of instructors used in the lectures varies. Most courses divide the lectures among the instructors, but one instructor can do all of them if necessary. A course with 20 to 24 students can get by with a course director, course coordinator, and ten instructors, but it would be wise to have two or three more instructors to provide some relief at the teaching and testing stations. A class of 36 to 40 students requires a total of at least 14 instructors for efficiency. Most instructors are needed the second day. Two evaluators are needed for each patient scenario station. The more scenario stations used, the quicker the second day is completed. Since all the skill stations must be taught, a minimum of nine instructors is needed the first day (thirteen are recommended). One of the advantages of having all of the skill stations and testing done the second day is that fewer instructors are needed the first day.

When selecting instructors, remember that some people are good at lectures, others are good at practical skills teaching, and a few are good at both. Try to make assignments that correspond to the instructor's abilities. Local faculty should be used whenever possible. The greatest cost involved in a BTLS course is the cost for out-of-town instructors. Many instructors serve without pay, but out-of-town instructors should have their expenses paid. Although we prefer having the same instructors for both days, it is not absolutely necessary, as some people have only one day available to give.

In unusual circumstances a physician or other EMS provider (EMT, registered nurse, nurse practitioner, or physician assistant) who has not taken the instructor course may help teach a BTLS course. However, this may be done only with the permission of the chapter BTLS medical director or committee. This requirement is necessary to maintain the high quality of certified courses.

Instructors should all be consistent. There are two ways to stop inconsistencies. One way is to cover all of the normal inconsistencies in the instructor meeting prior to the course. The other is to monitor each lecture to catch such inconsistencies.

During the selection of instructors, you must ensure that at least four of your instructors are very good at patient assessment demonstrations. A way to ensure this is to have those particular instructors demonstrate the skills to the coordinator prior to the course.

Selecting Models

Since both acting ability and hard work are required of the models, you should use your best judgment when selecting them. They will be required to submit to being examined, handled, extricated, splinted, and strapped for several hours. They should be paid for their efforts. Since they will always have to have their chests examined, it is less embarrassing to have all male models except for those scenarios that call for a female. All models should be furnished old clothes or asked to wear clothes that they do not mind having ruined (it is a good idea to have clothes made up with Velcro fasteners so they can be pulled apart for exam and then easily stuck back together). Females should be warned to wear bathing suits under their clothes. Since the models will learn a lot about trauma care, it is recommended that EMTs or EMT students be used for this role. Students who are enrolled in the BTLS course should not be used for models except for minor skills such as traction splinting or helmet removal. The weight and age of a model should be a consideration. Models who are too heavy may cause injuries to your students, and models who are too young may have too short an attention span to last through a scenario.

Selecting the Site

Selection of the appropriate site is the responsibility of the course coordinator and medical director. They should inspect the facility to determine the adequacy of the following:

1. Large lecture room to accommodate both students and faculty. The standard ratio for a classroom is one person per 15 square feet. In other words, a 750-square-foot classroom would comfortably fit 50 people.
2. An adequate number of tables and chairs.
3. Find out how many windows are in the classroom. If there are windows, they will need to have shades so the screen can be seen.
4. Are heating and air conditioning functional?
5. Ten rooms or spaces to accommodate students and equipment for the skill stations.
6. Eight to twelve rooms or spaces to accommodate students and equipment for the patient scenarios. (*Note:* These rooms should be near each other to prevent the students from meandering through the halls of the building and pausing to socialize.)
7. Equipment security.
8. On-site meal functions.
9. Privacy, which will prevent distractions to the students and shock to the casual passerby.

BTLS courses have been adequately taught in motels, churches, junior colleges, hospitals, scout camps, and EMS training facilities.

If you are teaching at another facility you should inspect the site if possible. You will also need the name of a responsible contact person and must see that they get the precourse information for the students. You also must be sure the instructors get a map of the location to include local restaurants.

Equipment

Equipment should be assessed and inventoried two to three weeks prior to the course. When borrowing equipment, the equipment manager (see Delegating Tasks, page 20) should use a detailed checklist to see that *all* equipment is properly identified as to ownership and condition. Both before and after the course, it is advantageous to have staging areas, where equipment is grouped by source. This area should have limited access and should be used to inventory and label equipment carefully. Any borrowed equipment should be returned cleaned and in good repair. This step is often a neglected item at the close of the course because of the fatigue and the natural urge to "wrap it up and go home." The equipment list is lengthy, and a great deal of time is required for determining needs and inventory. Equipment needs will vary from course to course, depending on the number of students and the patient assessment situations chosen. There is an equipment list with each skill station. There is a master equipment list that follows, but there is always some variation in equipment needs depending on the assessment scenarios chosen. Though not listed, a large coffeepot is an essential item.

The following are sources for equipment:

1. Regional EMS offices
2. Local EMT training departments
3. Hospitals
4. Prehospital provider services

Master Equipment List

The amount of equipment needed for the second day of the course will depend on how many patient assessment scenario stations you set up. To determine your equipment needs, list the total of the equipment that is required for the patient assessment scenario stations you intend to include in the course. Check that against the amount of equipment needed for the first day. You will usually need more backboards, oxygen masks, bag-valve devices, blood pressure (BP) cuffs, stethoscopes, and trauma boxes. Assess and inventory the complete equipment list two to three weeks prior to the course.

The following master equipment list is itemized by category. It covers equipment needed for the skill stations the first day but not the patient scenarios (each has its own equipment list) the second day:

Category	Item	Quantity
Skill Station 1—Basic and Advanced Airway Management		
	Exam gloves (large nonsterile)	1 box
	Goggles/face shield	2
	Mannequin, trauma or ACLS (optional)	1
	Airway mannequin—Adult	4
	—Pediatric	2
	Silicone lubricant spray (cans)	2
	Portable suction machine with charger	2
	Manual suction device (optional)	2
	Tonsil tip	2

Suction tubes (14–18 Fr.)	2
Tongue blades	10
Oropharyngeal airways (set)	2
Nasopharyngeal airways (set)	2
Pocket mask (with supplemental oxygen nipple)	2
Adult bag-valve device/reservoir	2
Pediatric bag-valve device/reservoir	2
Adult face mask (#4–5)	2
Pediatric face masks (#1–3)	2
Oxygen cylinder with regulator	2
Stand for oxygen cylinder	2
Oxygen tubing	2
Nasal cannula	2
Non-rebreather mask	2
Pulse oximeter	1 or 2
Stethoscope	4
Endotracheal tubes 7–9	2 ea.
Endotracheal tube 3.5 Fr.	2
Stylet (adult, pediatric)	2 ea.
Lighted stylet (optional)	1
10-cc syringe	2
Bottle of water	1
Combitube (optional)	2
Laryngoscope	2
Spare batteries	4
Curved blades #3–4	2 ea.
Straight blades #2–3 and #1	2 ea.
Spare bulbs	1 ea.
CO_2 detector (optional)	1
Esophageal detection device (optional)	2

Skill Station 2—Short Backboard/KED/Rapid Extrication

Live model	2
Rigid cervical collar (assorted sizes or adjustable)	2 ea.
Long backboard with straps	2
Short backboard with straps (optional)	1
Head or cervical immobilization device	2
KED or similar vest-type extrication device	1
Padding	1
Tape	2
Elastic wrap (ace)	1
Chair	4
Vehicle (optional)	1 or 2

Skill Station 3—Traction Splints

Live model	2
Padding	2
Tape	1
Thomas splint	1

Sager or hare splint	1
Tongue blades (for Spanish windless)	10
Cravat	1

Skill Station 4—Helmet Management/Log-Roll/Long Backboard

Live model	2
Rigid cervical collar (assorted sizes or adjustable)	2 ea.
Long backboard with straps	1
Reeve sleeve (optional)	1
Miller body splint (optional)	1
Vacuum backboard (optional)	1
Head or cervical immobilization device	1
Padding	1
Tape	4 rolls
Elastic wrap (ace)	1
Motorcycle helmet (full face)	1
Football helmet with face protector	1
Shoulder pads	1 set
Open face helmet	1

Skill Station 5—Chest Decompression/IV/IO

Central line (E-J) mannequin (optional)	1
IO mannequin	1
Decompression mannequin	1
(some of the older models do not work with the anterior approach)	
Artificial tension pneumothorax (optional)	
Section of pork ribs at least 12" by 12"	1
Small trailer wheel inner tube	1
Valve core remover	1
Hand, foot, or electric air pump	1
8-fluid-ounce bottle of tire puncture sealer	2
Roll of plastic wrap	1
Roll of duct tape of foam latex tape	1
One-way valve	
Asherman chest seal (optional)	1
Flutter valve #1	2
Plastic 10-cc syringe	2
Penrose drain	2
Flutter valve #2	20
Rubber condom (insert the decompressing needle through the condom)	
10-cc syringe	6
14-, 18-, 20-ga over-the-needle catheter	20 ea.
IV tubing (optional)	3
Small container of water (optional)	1
Paper towels	2 rolls
20-cc syringes	2
Chicken legs (optional)	6–12

| Betadine solution (4-oz bottle) | 1 |
| Intraosseous needles | 6 |

Skill Station 6—Patient Assessment (2 Stations)

Exam gloves (large)	2 boxes
Trauma Box (jump kit—see below)	2
Monitor-defibrillator (optional)	2
MAST (optional)	2
Live model	2
Adult bag-valve device/reservoir	2
Rigid cervical collar (size to fit your model)	2
Long backboard with straps	2
Head immobilization device	2
Padding	2
Moulage kit or white tape and red felt-tip pen	1
Trauma box (jump kit)	
You will need two trauma boxes the first day. The second day you will need one for each patient assessment scenario. Each trauma box should contain the following:	
Stethoscope	1
Blood pressure cuff	1
Pocket mask	1
4-inch elastic wrap (ace)	4
6-inch elastic wrap (ace)	2
Kerlix rolls	4
4 × 4 gauze pads (unsterile)	20
Wide adhesive tape	1 roll
One-inch adhesive tape	3 rolls
IV tubing	2 sets
Oxygen mask or nasal prongs	1

Miscellaneous

Clipboards	12
Pencils	30
Moulage kit (see Chapter 9)	1
Spray bottles with glycerin-water mix	3
35-mm slide projector	1–2
Spare bulb for projector	1–2
Pointer	1
Cloth towels	8
Wide adhesive tape	10 rolls
Blankets	2
Felt-tip pens (red and black)	2 ea.

Meals

BTLS is such an intensive learning course that convenient on-site lunches are desirable in order to save time. The advantages of on-site meals include the following:

1. They keep the students in contact with other students and faculty to foster the sharing of professional experience.

2. They keep the students in close proximity to the course for easier coordination.

3. They keep the amount of lost time to a minimum by eliminating waiting time and travel time for students.

The disadvantages of on-site meals are as follows:

1. Increased course registration fees to cover the cost of meals

2. Inability to satisfy everyone's gourmet tastes

On-site meals need to be cost-effective and simple. Allowing the students to wander to restaurants and stand in line to be served is a hindrance to course completion but at times necessary. If you cannot provide on-site meals, you should provide specific directions or maps to nearby restaurants.

Course Budget

One of the earliest headaches for the course coordinator is to establish the course budget. This needs to be one of the first considerations in planning a course because the course fee needs to be set early on. Several factors in a budget need to be considered:

1. Site rental
2. Mailings
   a. Precourse advertising
   b. Faculty invitation letters
   c. Faculty precourse mailings
   d. Student precourse mailings
   e. Student/faculty postcourse mailings
3. Student and instructor guides
4. Lunches for students, faculty, and models
5. Breaks for students, faculty, and models
6. Faculty stipends (if offered)
7. Faculty travel and lodging (if necessary to use out-of-town faculty)
8. Chapter/international assessment fees
9. Equipment
10. Miscellaneous
    a. Postage
    b. Photocopying
    c. Envelopes, paper, name tags, markers, and so on

Instructor Ready Book

The following was developed by Texas BTLS to help decrease the confusion in coordinating a BTLS course. The books are made in inexpensive three-ring binders. There is only one book per lecture, one book per skill station, and one book per testing scenario. Originally, building this bank of books takes a bit of work. You will need to do a lot of copying the first time you make them, but it will save you a lot of copying in future courses. You must keep track of these books, collecting and storing them between each course. However, it really pays off as you get ready for each course you coordinate.

Lecture Book

The following items are placed permanently in each lecture book:

1. A copy of the assigned lecture
2. Chapter objectives and key lecture points from Chapter 6 of the instructor's guide
3. Slide information from Chapter 6 of the instructor's guide
4. Test questions from the assigned lecture

At the beginning of the book, the following items are changed per course:

1. The letter of what is expected from instructors
2. Location and map
3. Class schedule

Skill Station Book

The following items are placed permanently in each skill station book:
1. A copy of the skills criteria from the student manual
2. A copy of the skills criteria from the instructor's guide
3. A list of equipment required for that particular skill station

At the beginning of the book, the following items are changed per course:

1. The letter of what is expected from instructors
2. Class schedule

Testing Scenario Book

The following are placed permanently in each testing scenario book:

1. Four copies of the scenario
   a. One for the instructor
   b. One for the moulage technician
   c. One for the model
   d. One to stay in the book if the others are lost
2. Twelve scenario testing check-off sheets
   (Some prefer different colored sheets for practice and testing)

The books should be numbered 1 through 12 (or however many are chosen) corresponding to the scenario in the instructor's guide.

Delegating Tasks

Staff support is needed in the following areas:

Correspondence—An efficient and organized secretary is invaluable in this area. Several mailings and even more rosters are involved. The secretary will make mailing lists and participant and faculty rosters and send confirmation notices. This person must have access to a copy machine since parts of the instructor's guide may need to be copied for the lectures and skill stations. There are also many schedules and rosters that must be sent to both faculty and students.

Equipment manager—One person should be assigned the task of keeping up with equipment. This is especially true at the end of the course when everyone is tired and ready to go home. If one person does not take responsibility for getting equipment cleaned, repaired, packaged, and returned, there will be equipment missing.

Timekeeper during the skill stations—There is a very tight schedule during the skill stations. There are only 30 minutes in which to practice a skill, prepare the room for the next group, and mobilize the present group toward their next station. One person should be delegated to notify each instructor five minutes before the end of the teaching period. This person, usually the coordinator, should then notify each instructor when the period is over. Unless monitored closely, skill stations tend to run overtime, with resultant schedule disruption and confusion.

Models—One person should be responsible for recruiting models for the skill stations (day one or two) and patient assessment (day two). This same person should coordinate makeup of the models. Models should be brought in at least two hours ahead of time in order to have their makeup applied (unless you are going to use felt-tip pen moulage). Failure to do this will always result in a delay of the afternoon session and will ensure a late finish on the day.

Makeup (moulage)—At least two people should be assigned the task of applying makeup and moulage to the models. They should be reminded that *simpler is better.* Complex moulage often falls off after the first session. The commercial rubber moulage is not as realistic but is very durable. Using a felt-tip pen to simply draw and label the injury (onto a piece of white tape that is stuck to the affected part) is also acceptable. The moulage coordinator should be prepared to make the rounds during the course to maintain the victims' moulage.

MASTER CHECKLIST

Precourse

Three Months in Advance

1. Select the target group of students with the director.
2. Decide if you are going to teach any optional material; students and instructors must be notified early so they are prepared (see Frequently Asked Questions). As a general rule, you should teach what is accepted technique in your area.
3. Select the site and date. Submit a request for course approval through the chapter BTLS office. This ensures that there are no scheduling or other conflicts.
4. Make initial faculty contact.
5. Establish a tentative budget for your course.

6. Once the course is approved, mail invitations/brochures to the target group of students.

7. Appoint an equipment manager and together take an inventory of the on-site equipment. Determine the needed equipment from the lists in the skill stations and patient assessment stations. Make initial contact for outside sources of equipment.

8. Visit the site and confirm dates. Order the menu for the meals, and arrange for refreshments at the breaks.

Two Months in Advance

1. Reserve the faculty and staff hotel/motel rooms in person to determine the adequacy of the accommodations. An evening meeting place at the hotel for the visiting faculty is advantageous. If lodgings are some distance away from the course site, maps should be provided.

2. Order the provider manuals.

3. Send faculty acknowledgment letters with course dates and reply cards for confirmation. To avoid misunderstanding, the introductory letter should state whether the faculty members are performing gratis, for reimbursement of expenses, or for a stated honorarium and reimbursement of some or all expenses.

4. Decide if you wish to sell and distribute BTLS novelty items (T-shirts, pins, etc.) Either order the supplies through your chapter office or photocopy the order form for use by the students.

One Month in Advance

1. Prepare the faculty roster and assignments.

2. Send faculty precourse letter. The following items should be sent to each faculty member:
   a. Acknowledgement letter
   b. A copy of the appropriate part of Chapter 3, Teaching Strategies: Guide for Instructors section of the instructor's guide (if your instructors do not have an instructor's guide)
   c. Slides and/or slide guide for scheduled lectures
   d. Agenda for lectures and practical sessions
   e. Location and floor plan of the facility where the course will be taught
   f. Faculty assignments for lecture, skill stations, and patient assessment stations
   g. Registration forms for hotel/motel accommodations (if applicable)

3. Confirm all hotel/motel reservations.

4. Prepare the student roster as candidates apply.

5. Prepare and mail acknowledgments to registrants. Include a precourse study packet as follows:
   a. BTLS textbook (unless the students have already purchased them).
   b. Pretest, answer sheet, and key.
   c. Tentative course schedule with a list of any optional skills to be taught. Make it clear to the students that they do not have to be responsible for optional skills that are not to be covered in a particular course.
   d. Map of course location to include area hotels.
   e. A copy of the Student's Guide section of the instructor's manual (see Appendix) or similar prepared handout.

6. Check the available equipment again with the equipment manager. Verify where the remainder of the equipment is to be obtained and who is transporting it.

7. Recruit models with the moulage coordinator.

Two Weeks in Advance

1. Prepare the final candidate roster.

2. Meet with the course director to check the following:
   a. Final schedule
   b. Equipment
   c. Facility

3. Prepare candidate packets:
   a. Welcome letter
   b. Group assignments
   c. Final agenda
   d. Rotation schedules
   e. Faculty roster—with work addresses (do not include home telephone numbers)
   f. Student roster—with work addresses (do not include home telephone numbers)
   g. Name tags

4. Make a final site visit:
   a. Confirm breaks and meals with caterers.
   b. Check rooming lists.
   c. Plan the layout of the rooms for skill stations and patient assessment stations.
   d. Make arrangements to open the doors at 6:30 A.M. in order to organize the equipment staging area and make the coffee.

5. Send confirmation letter to models. Specify clothing to wear, eating accommodations, reimbursement, meeting place, and times.

6. Photocopy the necessary pages from the instructor's guide to include
   a. Pages relevant to each instructor's skill station.
   b. Pages relevant to each instructor's patient assessment station.
   c. Posttest and answer sheet for each student (with extras). This will come from the BTLS chapter office.
   d. Patient assessment grade sheets (10 to 15 copies for each station).
   e. Equipment list for each skill station and patient assessment station with the numbers of the skill station and patient assessment station to be taped to the door for the equipment manager.
   f. The various forms (such as the course evaluation form).

7. If you plan to photograph the students for identification, prepare 8.5 x 11–inch papers with the student's name printed with a dark marker.

The Day Before the Course

1. Take all equipment to the staging area of the facility. Inventory and properly label it. Secure the area.

2. Set up, inventory, and check all audiovisual equipment. You should have two 35-mm projectors with extra carousels, screen, 115-volt extension cord, slide advance remote control with extension, and microphone for soft-voiced speakers if the size of the room requires it. Borrow an extra set of slides if possible. Some instructors forget to bring their slides. Arrange and check a VCR and TV if using video format for any presentations.

3. At the precourse faculty meeting (usually the night prior to registration) give the faculty their packets. Include an agenda, station locations, selected scenarios, assignments, and final roster. Review the game plan for the weekend, including the following:

a. Meals and meetings.

b. Final agenda with changes noted.

c. Student registrants, reviewing backgrounds (prehospital, nursing, industrial, military).

d. Plan for management of equipment.

e. Skill stations.

f. Grading criteria and retest policy for patient assessment.

g. Ground rules for student team member roles.

h. Plan for setting up skill stations and distribution of equipment.

i. Reminder that the slides are to be turned in immediately after the lecture. Find out if any have forgotten to bring their slides.

First Day of the Course

1. Arrive early with the equipment manager and moulage coordinator. Verify thermostat settings, posting of outside signs, room assignments, equipment distribution, and model preparation, and make coffee.

2. Verify proper functioning of audiovisual equipment and set up registration desk.

3. Register participants and collect their pretests.

4. Take instant photographs, if possible, to assist in identifying students during the course and at the closing faculty meeting. (The cheapest way to photograph students is to take photos with a digital camera and print the photos on your printer). If a video camera is available, you may record each student on a videotape and prepare a typed list of the students in the order in which they appear. At the postcourse faculty meeting the students should be discussed in the order that they appear on the tape. If you decide to use one of these methods, please explain to the students that the only purpose of the photos or videos is to help the faculty identify the students.

5. Line up the lecturers; introduce the first speaker, make sure the second one is ready, and so on. Collect the slides immediately after each lecture and take note of any slides that are missing or damaged. If a scheduled lecturer does not show up on time, you may substitute another lecture (it is a good idea to ask all lecturers to be present at the beginning of the course) or have one of the other faculty members give the scheduled lecture.

6. During the morning lecture session, the other faculty members should set up their skill stations and inventory their equipment. It is best to do this the night before, but providing equipment security often prevents this.

7. Check to be sure that the models arrive in time to be moulaged before the patient assessment skill stations.

8. Have a brief faculty meeting to review goals and procedures before beginning the skill stations. This may be done during lunch, but it is better for the faculty to have lunch with the students. Students are much more likely to ask questions of the faculty at this time.

9. Assign someone to notify each instructor five minutes before the end of each skill station teaching period. This person should then notify each instructor when the period is over. You must keep the stations on time. Any station that runs over its scheduled time will back up the whole schedule.

10. Enlist the support of the faculty to tear down the skill stations and distribute the equipment to the patient assessment stations. Extra equipment should be stored in the equipment staging area. Maintaining equipment security may prevent you from distributing equipment until the second day.

The Second Day of the Course

1. Arrive early with the equipment manager and moulage coordinator. Confirm the room assignments, verify the functioning of the audiovisual equipment, and make the coffee.

2. Greet the students, correct any registration deficiencies from the first day, and have the continuing education forms filled out, signed, and collected.

3. Line up the lecturers; introduce the first speaker, make sure the second one is ready, and so on. Collect the slides immediately after each lecture and take note of any slides that are missing or damaged.

4. Direct the moulage coordinator to take charge of the models and their moulage.

5. Have faculty members set up their patient assessment stations and inventory their equipment.

6. Verify that the written examination room is set up with answer sheets and pencils. A monitor should be assigned to the room. Tests should be graded immediately by the monitor.

7. Verify that the instructors close their stations for lunch and that food is brought to the models. A secluded classroom for the models is appropriate. Someone should be assigned to take refreshments to the models during the afternoon.

8. Set up a collection area during testing. Collect the patient assessment evaluations and collate them with the written tests and photographs.

9. Arrange with a testing instructor, student, and course director for the retest of students who fail their first practical test.

10. See that course evaluation forms are available for the students to fill out before they leave.

11. Pass out continuing education forms if not already done.

12. Direct the instructors and the equipment manager to break down the patient assessment stations. Bring all of the equipment to the staging area. The equipment manager should stay at the staging area to verify that the equipment, which is leaving the area, is going with the appropriate person. Borrowed equipment should be cleaned and repaired before returning.

13. Arrange for the postcourse faculty meeting:
    a. Have available the collated student records for the faculty to review.
    b. Appoint a recorder to document the results of the written exam, practical practice, practical test, practical retest (if any), and final faculty decision, using the form provided.
    c. Collect comments from the faculty about the course and teaching material. How could they be improved?
    d. Distribute the faculty stipends (if any).
    e. Pay the models (unless other arrangements have been made).

14. Verify with the equipment manager that the equipment has been distributed to the appropriate departing faculty.

15. Prepare and distribute the following to those students who have waited in order to get their grades immediately:
    a. Participant scores
    b. BTLS cards
    c. Letter of attendance (for students who failed the course)

The Day After the Course

Take a breather for a job well done.

One Week After the Course

1. Prepare and mail, if not distributed at the close of the course, the following:
   a. Participant scores.
   b. BTLS cards—It is your (and the chapter's) responsibility to see that the students get their cards in a timely manner. The day of the course is preferred, but under no circumstances should it be longer than 90 days.
   c. Letters of attendance (for students who failed the course).
   d. Thank-you letter to faculty.

2. Check all invoices and bills prior to payment. Make a course financial statement.

3. Hold a staff critique.

4. You should mail the following for postcourse audit to your chapter BTLS office (this may vary from chapter to chapter; check with your chapter office):
   a. Any borrowed course materials (slides, equipment, and so on).
   b. An updated student roster. Keep a copy for your files.
   c. An updated faculty/staff roster. Keep a copy for your files.
   d. The completed chapter and/or international course registration forms with the appropriate checks made out to the chapter or international BTLS office as directed by your chapter. These forms are used to compile the statistics of BTLS providers, instructor candidates, and instructors internationally. In some chapters your BTLS cards will not be sent until the student fees are paid to the chapter and international offices. It is your (and the chapter's) responsibility to see that the students get their cards in a timely manner. The day of the course is preferred, but under no circumstances should it be longer than 90 days.

5. Inventory, clean, repair, and return all equipment to the proper local facilities. Thank all individuals who provided support for the course

SKILL STATION 1

BASIC
AND
ADVANCED
AIRWAY
MANAGEMENT

SKILL STATION 2

SHORT BACKBOARD

KED

RAPID EXTRICATION

SKILL STATION 3

TRACTION SPLINTS

SKILL STATION 4

PATIENT ASSESSMENT AND MANAGEMENT

SKILL STATION 5

CHEST DECOMPRESSION

IV ACCESS

IO ACCESS

SKILL STATION 6

HELMET MANAGEMENT

LOG-ROLL

LONG BACKBOARD

STATION 7

PATIENT

ASSESSMENT
AND
MANAGEMENT

TESTING
STATION

1

TESTING
STATION

2

TESTING
STATION

3

TESTING
STATION

4

TESTING
STATION

5

TESTING
STATION

6

TESTING
STATION

7

TESTING STATION

8

TESTING STATION

9

TESTING
STATION

10

3
Teaching Strategies: Guide for Instructors

ROLES AND RESPONSIBILITIES

The original Oath of Hippocrates required the medical practitioner to swear to teach the art of medicine to others. This concept is still very important. Medicine is not just a trade or craft; it is an art, and we as practitioners must give something back to the art to improve it constantly. Teaching is a wonderful way to accomplish this. Teaching is extremely important in that our influence may pass from generation to generation, doing good or harm long after we are gone. Donating our precious off time to teach others how to save lives is in the highest traditions of medicine.

BTLS instructors are responsible for knowing all of the BTLS material in order to present their assigned topic in a simple and easily understood manner that ties in with the other parts of the BTLS method. It is just as important that, whenever possible, the instructors remain available to the students for the purpose of answering questions and providing individual help. This includes eating and socializing with the students. Often, students will not ask the questions they really want to ask until they know the instructor and feel confident that the instructor will not ridicule them. It is understood that there will be times that you can be present only long enough to present your material, but, if at all possible, you should be present for the entire course.

BTLS is a composite of accepted and new (optional) techniques for the care of trauma patients. If you do not agree with any of the material, you should make your thoughts known to the chapter BTLS chairperson or committee. BTLS is constantly being reviewed, and feedback is welcome. Changes will be made whenever they are judged to be an improvement over existing techniques. Feedback should be directed to the chapter affiliate faculty or chapter medical director, not to the students. It you teach material in conflict to the text, you will only confuse the students, so if you feel that you cannot teach the material as written, please do not agree to teach.

The goal of all instructors of BTLS is to teach every student enough to pass the course and thus improve the quality of prehospital trauma care.

TEACHING METHODOLOGY

Learning is a relatively permanent change in behavior that comes about as a result of a planned experience. Teaching is a method of attaining this desired change. We are involved in teaching adults, most of who are already practicing as EMTs or nurses. To gain their cooperation in the learning process, we must

1. Convince them that there is a gap between the level at which they wish to perform and the level that they are actually performing.

2. Help them to attain the desired level of performance.

To accomplish this, the learner must accept the performance goals as personal goals and must also accept a share of the responsibility for attaining those goals. This is all just a way of saying that it is almost impossible to teach something to someone who does not feel the need to know the material. Good instructors must not only know the material and how to explain it, they must be able to "sell" the "need to know" to the student. BTLS instructors should accept the philosophy that they are a team with the student and their goal is to help every student attain the desired level of performance before the course is over. The practice of medicine is unique in that poor performance does not just lead to a poor product; it may result in the loss of life. We should consider our students as family and be willing to go the extra mile to help them learn. The instructor who takes pride in how many students fail has no business in medicine or education.

Effective teachers

1. Are polite

2. Are pleasant in their interactions

3. Call students by name

4. Give praise and positive feedback

5. Involve students in decision making

6. Do not ignore, belittle, or harass students

7. Make reasonable demands on students

8. Are businesslike and warm

9. Are knowledgeable about their subject

10. Use gestures and movement (are not "stiff")

11. Make few errors

In general, lectures are effective ways to transfer information but alone are less effective for assuring long-term retention. Hands-on practice with a caring, interactive instructor is one of the best ways to assure retention. Therefore, lectures must be succinct, to the point, and as free as possible of incorrect information. If the lecture runs over its appointed time frame, there is probably information presented that will not be remembered anyway.

Learning proceeds most smoothly when material is somewhat new or challenging yet relatively easy for the students to relate to their existing knowledge.

PRESENTATION OF LECTURES

1. **Make a good opening.** Use the opening to tell the students what you are going to discuss, why it is important to them, and what they should learn from the lecture.

2. **Make a good presentation of the material.**
   a. Avoid reading (slides or notes) or reciting; it is boring, and students will retain only 50 percent even with the best of audiovisual aids
   b. Use a variety of styles (questions, thought-provoking statements, etc.) when you lecture:
      • What are the ABCs of trauma?

- If a negative pressure inside the thorax accomplishes inspiration, what will happen if there is a gaping hole in the thorax?
- If shock causes this catecholamine response, what symptoms should we look for in the shocky patient?
- Why do we no longer hyperventilate the head injury patient?
- What injuries would you expect in this patient who was just struck from the passenger's side?

  c. Highlight the important points in your opening and closing remarks: "This is what we are going to discuss, . . . this is what we are saying, . . . this is what we just discussed."

  d. Relate the (action) slides to your experiences and the experiences of the students:
- This is the picture of the ankle of the man we picked up last week.
- This is the sequence of slides of the fire truck crash they had in Port Huron shortly before we visited there.
- This chest X-ray shows an injury just like the one in the patient you brought to the hospital last week.

  e. Do not try to cover too many points. Teach key concepts.

3. **Make a good closing.** Review the objectives that you outlined in your opening. Briefly bring everything together in a way that relates to those objectives.

IMPORTANT LECTURE PRESENTATION TOOLS

1. Eye contact:
   - Read your audience—get feedback.
   - Identify three to five students near the corners of the class and talk to them.
   - Occasionally speak to people who are not paying attention.

2. Movement:
   - Don't get stuck behind the podium or audiovisual equipment.
   - Moving leisurely around the room keeps the students' attention, especially when getting close to them.
   - Avoid distracting the class with pacing, repetitive movements, or inappropriate wardrobe; they may spend more time looking at what you are doing or wearing than listening to what you are saying.

3. Voice:
   - Avoid distractive, repetitive words (uh, y'know, well, OK).
   - Vary your voice tone, volume, and speed.
   - Communicate important points by emphasizing with voice quality.

Help the students pass the course.

SKILL STATIONS

Objective

Acquisition of the psychomotor skills necessary for the rapid assessment and treatment of the multiple traumatized patient.

To Prepare

The skill stations are the heart of the course. Time should be used efficiently so that every student can become proficient in the procedures. The instructors must rehearse the station well, including the model if appropriate. The instructor must learn what equipment is needed and see that it is available and set up correctly beforehand. There are many optional skills included in the manual. The students should be notified well in advance of the course which skills will be taught (see the section in Chapter 2 titled What Must Be Taught in a Certified BTLS Course).

First review the skill station from the student's perspective by reading the individual skill station in the student manual. Next review the skill station from the instructor's perspective in Chapter 6 of the instructor's guide. Do this in advance of the course so that on the day of the course you can use your time setting up and practicing your station.

Use the skill station as a complement to the lectures and not to repeat the information already presented. Use the skill station as a preparatory step to the patient assessment stations by explaining what is to be expected of students in the application of the skills they are reviewing or learning. It is imperative that the instructor knows the content of the patient assessment stations.

Presenting a Skill Station

- Do not lecture at the skill station.

- Do present the objectives of the skill station.

- Demonstrate the skill and talk through the skill, have the students talk through the skill, then have the students practice the skill to their and your satisfaction.

- Encourage comments and questions about the procedure while students are busy practicing the skill.

- Remain flexible. Offer comments and feedback in a caring and constructive fashion. Do not embarrass the student who has difficulty with the skill being taught.

- If there are two instructors at your station, predetermine and coordinate your expectations.

- Allow as much time as possible for extra practice. Encourage the students to return at the end of the day if necessary. Give/offer extra help to those who may need it.

Help the students pass the course.

PATIENT ASSESSMENT SCENARIO PRACTICE AND TESTING

The ability to assess and manage trauma patients rapidly is the goal of the BTLS course. This time of practice, teaching, and then testing is extremely important.

1. Review teaching methodology (pages 49–50).
2. Familiarize yourself with what the members of the team are allowed to do during practice and testing. Review the section titled How to Function as a Team (Chapter 9).
3. Review Chapters 2 and 3 in the BTLS textbook.
4. During the practice-teaching portion, use the full time allowed. Allow the students to proceed with as little interruptions or prompting as possible. When they have finished, quickly critique their performance, show them how to do it correctly, and then allow them to practice as time permits. Take into account local law and protocol.

5. During the testing portion you should not teach or prompt, and you should not discuss the scenario when the student finishes. Any questions are to be answered after the postcourse faculty meeting. As soon as one team finishes their test, you should immediately prepare for the next team's testing. It is a long afternoon; you must keep things moving.

6. You need two instructors for each assessment station. One instructor cannot both interact with the team and grade at the same time. One instructor should present the patient scenario and interact with the team. The other instructor should keep times and fill out the grade sheet. When the practice or test is over, the two instructors should discuss the performance and assign a grade.

7. Fill out the grade sheet:
   a. Write the team leader's name and the scenario number at the top.
   b. Mark whether it is a practice or test.
   c. Record the pertinent times as indicated.
   d. Check off each step as the team performs the assessment. Make pertinent notes and comments about problems or techniques (good and bad). Do not record unkind or jesting remarks; the students are allowed to review their grade sheets.
   e. Review the critical actions; determine an overall grade and document why the student received that grade.
   f. Sign the grade sheet. It is important at the postcourse faculty meeting to know who graded each student (final grades may be raised on the basis of practice performance).

HOW TO PRESENT THE SCENARIO TO THE STUDENT

1. The scenario should be presented in the hall outside the room so that the scene does not distract the students.

2. Have the students introduce themselves and give their profession, level of training, and type of work. Use the appropriate setting (prehospital, nursing, occupational health/industrial, military) based on the student's background and work setting.

3. Remind students that they have medical direction available on the radio.

4. Remind students that this is an interactive scenario and they must tell the instructor everything that they are doing, or you will assume that it was not done.

5. Ask students if they have any questions.

6. Dispatch the call as it would be dispatched in a real situation.

TEACHING VERSUS TESTING FORMATS

Teaching	*Testing*
Interact without obstructing education.	Interact for vital signs and medical direction only.
Imprint the BTLS method, but don't interrupt so often that you obstruct the learning process.	
Reinforce the team concept.	Continue the team concept during testing.
Allow a longer time for each station.	Allow a shorter time for each station.

Remind and guide students to:

- Perform ongoing exam if patient worsens (and every five minutes during transport).

- Address critical care aspects.
- Splint all fractures, dress all wounds at the appropriate time.
- Do a detailed exam.
- Call medical direction.

Avoid reminding students about patient care.
Test only!
Do not teach!
Do not prompt!

You must remain objective and consistent for all testing scenarios.

GRADING

Written Test

Students must receive a minimum of 74 percent to pass and 86 percent to be considered for instructor potential. Students who fail the written test but pass the patient assessment testing are allowed to retake the written test within 6 weeks.

Patient Assessment Scenarios

Grading is done by way of individual check-off gradesheets. The generic gradesheets have every step of the assessment listed in an acceptable order followed by common critical actions and grading criteria. There is room for some variation in the order of the steps listed in the gradesheet. Do not become excessively rigid in this grading; no one (including you) will perform assessment exactly as listed on the gradesheet. You must look at the overall performance of the team leader as well as how well the team members assist and then assign a grade, taking into account the listed grading criteria and critical actions. It is important to write notes on the gradesheet to justify the grade that you assign, especially if you fail the student. Remember that patient assessment grading is subjective. If you become excessively rigid, no one will do well. You must look at the overall performance, not each individual action, when assigning a grade. Students who fail patient assessment but pass the written test are usually retested immediately using a different patient scenario (but may be allowed to retest within 6 weeks if they wish) to pass the course. Students who fail the practical retest may, at a future date, retake the course at a reduced fee. Students who fail both the written and the patient assessment tests should retake the course.

4

Case Scenarios:
Teaching and Evaluation Stations

Each scenario has four settings from which to choose. Select the most appropriate setting for the team leader in your student group. Learning should easily transfer to real-life actions. Please ensure that the scenario is as realistic as possible for each individual to facilitate learning.

It is imperative that you memorize the information relevant to the scenario you will be delivering. Students expect to receive responses to their requests quickly to minimize their assessment time.

SCENARIO 1

Setting

EMS/Prehospital

A young male was struck near the pit area at a car racetrack. He is found lying semiprone at the side of the track.

Nursing/Medical

A young male was struck near the pit area at a car racetrack. You are staffing the medical tent at the race and arrive to find the patient lying semiprone at the side of the track.

Occupational Health/Industrial

A young male fell off a loading dock and was run over by a truck as it was backing into the dock. He is found lying semiprone by the dock.

Military

The patient is a young male soldier who was dared by fellow soldiers to sprint across a busy road before traffic approached. He is found lying semiprone at the side of the road.

History

> S—"I can't breathe. My chest and leg hurt."
> A—allergic to penicillin
> M—insulin
> P—diabetes
> L—does not remember
> E—"He drove right over me!"

Injuries

1. Tension pneumothorax on left side
2. Intra-abdominal bleeding
3. Fracture of the left femur
4. Scalp laceration
5. Hypoglycemia

Patient Instructions

You should be confused and disoriented. You are having difficulty breathing. Complain of pain when your abdomen is palpated or your left chest or upper left leg is examined.

Moulage Instructions

Apply contusions and abrasions of left chest and abdomen. Use trousers with a large tear in left thigh area. The left thigh should have a large bruise, or write "fractured femur" on a piece of white tape with a felt-tip pen and apply it to the left thigh. Apply some fake blood to an area of the scalp (fake blood mixed with KY jelly works well here—don't use on light-colored hair; it will stain). Simulate diaphoresis.

Instructor Information

Scene size-up—no danger, mechanism as described, no other patients
Initial assessment
   General impression: patient with potentially critical injuries
   LOC—responds to verbal stimuli but is confused
   Airway—clear and open
   Breathing—rapid with poor movement of air
   Ventilation instructions—should order oxygen and ventilatory assistance
   Circulation
      Pulses—present at the wrist, rapid
      Bleeding—blood in hair, no major bleeding
      Skin color, condition and temperature—cyanotic, clammy, and cool
Decision—rapid trauma survey due to mechanism and initial assessment
Rapid trauma survey
   Head—blood in hair, no active bleeding, no other wounds noted
   Neck—no DCAP-BTLS
      Trachea—possible slight deviation to the right
      Neck veins—distended
   Chest—Looking—contusions of left chest, no paradoxical movement
      Feeling—some crepitation and tenderness
      Listening—decreased breath sounds on the left, heart sounds—present but difficult to hear
      Percussion—hyperresonant on the left
   Abdomen—tender to palpation, slightly distended
   Pelvis—no DCAP-BTLS
   Extremities
      Upper legs—swelling, tenderness, deformity of left upper leg, normal PMS
      Scan of lower legs and arms—no injuries noted
   Exam of posterior—no DCAP-BTLS
   Decision—load and go, consider immediate decompression of tension pneumothorax, splint left femur when in ambulance, two IV lines
   History (obtain from the patient)—
   Vital signs—BP 80/50, pulse 150, respiration 36, temperature feels cool
   Neurological
      LOC—confused and abusive, won't follow commands
      Pupils—equal and reactive
      Sensory—normal
      Motor—normal
      GCS—(13) eyes—open spontaneously (4), verbal—confused (4), motor—localizes pain (5)

Detailed exam (should be done after transport)
   History and vital signs (after decompression) BP 100/60, pulse 110, respiration 30
   Neurological (after decompression)
      LOC—still confused and abusive, won't follow commands
      Pupils—unchanged
      Sensory—normal
      Motor—normal
      GCS—unchanged
      Fingerstick glucose—40 (if glucose is given, LOC improves to near normal)
   Head—blood in hair from scalp laceration, no Battle's sign or raccoon eyes, face shows no signs of trauma, no drainage from ears or nose

Airway—open and clear

Breathing—improved movement of air if tension pneumothorax has been decompressed, otherwise worsening respiration

Neck—no DCAP-BTLS

Trachea—midline if tension pneumothorax decompressed

Neck veins—flat if tension pneumothorax decompressed

Circulation—BP still 100/60, skin pale, cool, clammy

Chest—Looking—contusions of left chest, no paradoxical movement

Feeling—no instability, some crepitation and tenderness

Listening—decreased breath sounds on the left, heart sounds—easier to hear now

Percussion—no longer hyperresonant on the left if decompressed

Abdomen—more distended, more tender

Pelvis—do not examine again

Extremities

Upper—no injuries noted, good PMS

Lower—should have left leg in traction splint, good PMS

Ongoing exam

Subjective changes—if given glucose patient feels better now

Neurological

LOC—improved, almost normal if glucose has been given, no change if glucose not given

Pupils—equal and reactive

GCS—(15) eyes—4, verbal—5, motor—6

Airway—open and clear

Breathing—rate 30, much better movement of air if tension decompressed

Circulation

Blood pressure—110/70 if decompression and fluid bolus

Pulses—rate 110

Skin color, condition, temperature—pale, cool, diaphoretic

Neck—no change

Trachea—midline

Neck veins—flat

Chest—unchanged, heart sounds—normal

Abdomen—more distended, more tender

Focused assessment of injuries

Scalp—no further bleeding

Pneumothorax—as above

Abdomen—as above

Left femur fracture—good PMS

Hypoglycemia—should be resolved

Check interventions

Is oxygen hooked up and turned on?

Decompression needle still patent?

Are IVs running? Rate?

Traction splint on left leg? PMS still OK?

Cardiac monitor applied?

Pulse oximeter applied? 92 percent saturation

Dressing to scalp

SCENARIO 2

Settings

EMS/Prehospital

The team is called to a laboratory where an explosion has taken place. The male patient is just inside the door about 10 yards/9 meters from active burning. What is left of his shirt is smoldering.

History

> S—"I can't feel anything from the neck down. My mouth and nose burn."
> A—no allergies
> M—no medications
> P—no history of serious illness
> L—last meal 6 hours ago
> E—"I had just entered the lab when an explosion threw me across the room."

Nursing/Medical

EMS was called to a laboratory where an explosion had taken place. The male patient was just inside the door about 10 yards/9 meters from active burning. EMS is transporting and will arrive in 10 minutes.

History

> S—"I can't feel anything from the neck down. My mouth and nose burn."
> A—no allergies
> M—no medications
> P—no history of serious illness
> L—last meal 6 hours ago
> E— "I had just entered the lab when an explosion threw me across the room."

Occupational Health/Industrial

The team is called to a laboratory where an explosion has taken place. The male patient is just inside the door about 10 yards/9 meters from active burning. What is left of his shirt is smoldering.

History

> S—"I can't feel anything from the neck down. My mouth and nose burn."
> A—no allergies
> M—no medications
> P—no history of serious illness
> L—last meal 6 hours ago
> E—"I had just entered the lab when an explosion threw me across the room."

Military

You are in a battle zone and are called to the scene of a helicopter that has been hit by a rocket. The helicopter crashed and is burning. The door gunner was thrown clear.

History

> S—"I can't feel anything from the neck down. My mouth and nose burn."
> A—no allergies
> M—no medications
> P—no history of serious illness
> L—last meal 6 hours ago
> E—"We were coming in to land and everything exploded."

Injuries

1. Second- and third-degree burns of face, anterior chest, and both arms
2. Upper airway burns
3. Open fracture of left forearm
4. Cervical spine injury
5. Spinal shock

Patient Instructions

You should be found crumpled in an awkward position, alert, complaining in a hoarse voice that you cannot move. Complain that your mouth and nose are burning. Partway through the assessment, start yelling, "Get me out of here, I can't breathe!" Thereafter rapidly loose consciousness and respond only to painful stimulus.

Moulage Instructions

1. Apply burn moulage to face, chest, and arms.
2. Apply commercial open fracture moulage to left forearm or just write "broken arm" on a piece of white tape with a felt-tip pen and apply it to the left forearm.
3. A tiny bit of charcoal on the tongue will simulate intraoral burns.

Instructor Information

Scene size-up—except for the nursing scenario, the scene is unsafe with fire and smoke present. The military scenario has the added danger of being fired upon. Mechanism is explosion and burns. There are no other live patients.

Initial assessment

  General impression—or potential for critical injuries

  LOC—alert

  Airway—open, burns in mouth and nose

  Breathing—normal rate and quality

  Ventilation instructions—give oxygen

  Circulation:

    Pulses—present at the wrist, rate seems normal

    Bleeding—no active bleeding

    Skin color, condition and temperature—burns of face, chest, and arms, otherwise normal color, warm, and dry

Decision—rapid trauma survey due to mechanism and facial burns

Rapid trauma survey

   Head—scalp normal, burns of face with singed hairs in the nose and burns inside the mouth

   Neck—no DCAP-BLTS, blistering burns of the anterior neck

     Trachea—midline

     Neck veins—flat

   Chest—Looking—burns present on anterior chest, no movement of ribs during breathing

     Feeling—no crepitation, no tenderness, no sensation, no instability

     Listening—breath sounds bilateral and equal, heart sounds—normal

   Abdomen—soft, no tenderness, no sensation

   Pelvis—stable

   Extremities

     Upper legs—no sign of trauma, no movement or sensation

     Scan of lower legs and arms—open fracture of left forearm, good pulse, no sensation or movement

   Exam of posterior—no sign of trauma, no sensation

   Decision—load and go, watch for airway compromise, cool burns and cover with clean sheet, splint forearm, two IV lines

   History (obtain from the patient)

   Vital signs—BP 70/40, pulse 65, respiration 16–18, temperature warm

Detailed exam (should be done after transport)

   History and vital signs—after fluid bolus: BP 76/50, pulse 65, respiration 16–18, temperature warm

   Neurological

     LOC—normal

     Pupils—equal and reactive

     Sensory—none below the neck

     Motor—none below the neck, diaphragmatic breathing

   Head—scalp normal, burns of mouth and inside nose, no drainage from nose or ears, no Battle's sign or raccoon eyes

   Airway—swelling of the lips and mouth, stridor when breathing if not already intubated. If student attempts oral intubation, tell him/her that the patient is gagging too much to intubate. Student should explain to the patient why intubation is needed. May perform nasotracheal intubation. or RSI

   Breathing—if intubated, rate 24, assistance not required

   Neck—tender lower neck, can feel step-off

     Trachea—midline

     Neck veins—flat

   Circulation—skin still warm and dry where not burned, no bleeding

   Chest—Looking—burns present on anterior chest, no movement of ribs during breathing

     Feeling—no crepitation, no tenderness, no sensation, no instability

     Listening—breath sounds bilateral and equal, heart sounds—normal

   Abdomen—unchanged

   Pelvis—no further exam

   Extremities

     Upper—unchanged, good pulse

     Lower—unchanged, good pulse

Decision—intubate if not already done, fluid bolus, may use PASG, splint arm if not already done

Ongoing Exam

  Subjective changes—patient can't speak due to being intubated

  Neurological

    LOC—awake, follows commands, can't speak due to endotracheal tube (ET)

    Pupils—equal and reactive

    Motor and sensory—unchanged

  Airway—should be intubated, if not, severe stridor

  Breathing—diaphragmatic but normal

  Circulation

    Blood pressure—80/50

    Pulses—rate 65

    Skin color, condition, and temperature—warm and dry where not burned

  Neck—unchanged

    Trachea—midline

    Neck veins—flat

  Chest—clear bilaterally, heart sounds—normal

  Abdomen—not distended, no sensation

  Focused assessment of injuries

    Burns—unchanged

    Fracture of left forearm—still has good pulse

    Upper airway burns—should be intubated

    Cervical spine injury—unchanged

    Spinal shock—unchanged

  Check interventions

    Is oxygen hooked up and turned on?

    ET tube in correct position?

    Are IVs running and at correct rate?

    Splint in good position, pulse OK?

    Dressing on open fracture blood soaked?

    Cardiac monitor applied?

    Pulse oximeter applied? 92 percent saturation

SCENARIO 3

Setting

EMS/Prehospital

The patient is a young male who is found in an alley. A police officer states that the patient is a known criminal who has been attacked. There is no other history available.

Nursing/Medical

A young male is brought to the emergency department entrance and thrown out of a moving car. Your attending physician has gone to eat, and her beeper is not working.

Occupational Health/Industrial

There has been a strike by the local union. There has been some violence and threats. Shots were heard, and the watchman found one of the employees lying in the parking lot. He appears to have been beaten and shot.

Military

You are in a battlefield situation. You have been called to get an injured soldier who is in a foxhole following hand-to-hand combat.

History

Not available

Injuries

1. Closed head injury with dilated pupil on right
2. Fracture of left femur
3. Gunshot wound of left forearm and right leg
4. Stab wound of lower back

Patient Instructions

You should respond only to pain. During the rapid trauma survey and the detailed exam, you should withdraw to pain. During the ongoing exam, you should localize to pain.

Moulage Instructions

If you use the Med-E-Train™ mannequin, the injuries are already present except for the stab wound in the back. Use a red felt-tip pen to write "stab wound" on a piece of white tape. Place the tape on the patient's back. You may also use one of the "Crash Kelly™" series mannequins for this scenario. If you use a live model you will have to moulage the injuries or use the felt-tip pen and tape method.

Instructor Information

Scene size-up—the scene is safe in all of the scenarios except the military. The soldier will have to be moved to a safe place for evaluation. There are no other patients.

Initial assessment
  General impression—potential for critical injuries
  LOC—withdraws to pain
  Airway—open
  Breathing—rate slow, depth normal
  Ventilation instructions—assist ventilation with oxygen
    Pulses—rapid, present at the neck but not at the wrist
    Bleeding—from right ear, left forearm, right lower leg
    Skin color, condition and temperature—pale, cool, clammy
Decision—Rapid trauma survey due to mechanism and initial assessment
Rapid trauma survey
  Head—bleeding from right ear, Battle's sign on right, and several contusions of face and scalp
  Neck—no obvious injury
    Trachea—midline
    Neck veins—flat
  Chest—Looking—no DCAPP-BTLS
        Feeling—table, no crepitation
        Listening—breath sounds present and equal, heart sounds—normal
  Abdomen—no obvious injury
  Pelvis—stable
  Extremities
    Upper legs—displaced femur fracture on left, pulses present both legs
    Scan of lower legs and arms—bleeding gunshot wound of right lower leg and left forearm, pulses present
  Exam of posterior—stab wound of the back, still bleeding
  Decision—load and go (head injury, shock, abdominal injury), intubate, two IV lines, traction splint left femur, dressing to right leg and left arm and back
  History—unable to obtain
  Vital signs—BP 70 systolic, pulse 140, respiration 8, temperature cool and clammy
  Neurological
    LOC—withdraws to pain
    Pupils—left 5 mm, right 8 mm, reaction to light: left normal, right sluggish
    Sensory—no response
    Motor—withdraws to pain
    GCS—(6) eyes: do not open—1, verbal: none—1, motor: withdraws to pain—4

Detailed exam (should be done after transport)
  History and vital signs—after IV fluid bolus: BP 100/70, pulse 110, patient should be intubated and ventilated with 100% oxygen at a rate of about 12–15 breaths per minute
  Neurological
    Unchanged from above
  Head—multiple contusions, no blood or fluids from nose, blood coming from left ear, Battle's sign present on right
  Airway—should be intubated
  Breathing—should be assisting at rate of 12–15 breaths per minute (one breath every 5 seconds)
  Neck—unchanged
    Trachea—midline
    Neck veins—flat
  Circulation—bleeding should be controlled, skin pale, cool, clammy

Chest—Looking—no DCAPP-BTLS
      Feeling—stable, no crepitation
      Listening—breath sounds present and equal, heart sounds—normal
Abdomen—unchanged
Pelvis—do not examine again
Extremities
    Upper—should have dressing on wound, weak pulses
    Lower—should have splint on left leg and dressing on right leg, weak pulses

Ongoing exam
    Subjective changes—patient unconscious
    Neurological
        LOC—localizes to pain
        Pupils—unchanged from above
        GCS—(7) improved from above, eyes: do not open—1, verbal: none—1, motor: localizes to
          pain—5
    Airway—should be intubated
    Breathing—rate 8/min when not ventilated—should be ventilated at a rate of 12–15 breaths/min
    Circulation
        Blood pressure—110/60 if IV fluids, 50 systolic if no fluids
        Pulses—rate 50–60
        Skin color, condition, temperature—pale, cool, diaphoretic
    Neck—unchanged
        Trachea—midline
        Neck veins—flat
    Chest—unchanged, heart sounds—normal
    Abdomen—unchanged
    Focused assessment of injuries
        Closed head injury—still has drainage from ear and dilated pupil, LOC is slightly improved
        Fractured femur—still has pulse,
        Gunshot wounds to forearm and leg—no further bleeding, still has pulse
        Stab wound of lower back—do not log-roll just to check unless blood is running out from
          under the patient
    Check interventions
        Is oxygen hooked up and turned on?
        Is the ET tube still in the trachea?
        Are you ventilating at the correct rate?
        Are IVs running at correct rate?
        Is the leg still correctly splinted?
        Are the dressings on arm and leg blood soaked?
        Is any blood coming from under the patient?
        Cardiac monitor applied? Sinus bradycardia
        Pulse oximeter applied? 98 precent saturation

SCENARIO 4

Setting

EMS/Prehospital

There has been a head-on collision of a sports car with a power pole. The unrestrained driver is still in the vehicle.

Nursing/Medical

A young adult male is brought to your emergency department in the back seat of a two-door car. He was found unconscious sitting behind the wheel of his car after colliding with a power pole. The steering wheel was broken and the windshield was knocked out. The people who brought the patient in do not know him. Your attending physician is with a critical patient and cannot help you at this time.

Occupational Health/Industrial

A truck loaded with crates backs into an employee, pinning him chest high against a concrete wall. The truck has been moved and a forklift has lifted the crates to allow access to the patient.

Military

There has been a head-on collision between a Humvee and a Bradley. The unrestrained driver is still in the Humvee.

History

Not available

Injuries

1. Sternal fracture
2. Myocardial contusion
3. Intra-abdominal bleeding
4. Concussion

Patient Instructions

Respond only to pain (localize). Moan with pain when your chest or abdomen is palpated.

Moulage Instructions

Apply contusions to forehead and sternum (see moulage techniques). Simulate shock.

Instructor Information

Scene size-up—for prehospital setting: power lines are down on the car. The gas tank has ruptured and is leaking. If the student tries to get the patient out of the car without calling the power company, tell him that he is electrocuted and must start over. If he elects to call the power company, tell him they have just arrived on the scene and have turned off the power and removed the lines. When the team approaches the vehicle (prehospital and military setting), tell them that the back of the vehicle has just burst into flames. If the team does not extricate by the rapid emergency extrication method, tell them that they have all burned up and must start over. Nursing and industrial settings have safe scenes. There are no other patients.

Initial assessment
  General impression—potential for critical injuries
  LOC—does not respond to voice but localizes to pain
  Airway—open, gag reflex present
  Breathing—normal rate and depth
  Ventilation instructions—give oxygen, assist ventilation as needed
  Circulation:
    Pulses—present at the wrist, seems a little fast
    Bleeding—no external bleeding noted
    Skin color, condition, and temperature—normal
  Decision—rapid trauma survey due to mechanism and exam
Rapid trauma survey
  Head—contusion of forehead
  Neck—no response to palpation, no injuries noted
    Trachea—midline
    Neck veins—flat
  Chest—Looking—contusion over sternum, otherwise normal
    Feeling—crepitance over sternum and anterior ribs, moans with pain when sternum and anterior ribs are palpated
    Listening—breath sounds present and equal, heart sounds—normal, but slightly irregular
  Abdomen—distended and painful moans when palpated
  Pelvis—stable and nontender
  Extremities
    Upper legs—normal
    Scan of lower legs and arms—normal
  Exam of posterior—normal
  Decision—load and go, two IV lines, monitor heart, monitor for need to intubate
  History (unable to obtain)
  Vital signs—BP 80/60, pulse 130, respiration 20, temperature normal
  Neurological
    LOC—localizes pain
    Pupils—5 mm, equal and reactive
    Sensory—localizes to pain
    Motor—moves all extremities to pain
    GSC—(8) eyes—open to pain (2), verbal—none (1), motor—localizes (5)

  Detailed Exam (should be done after transport)
  History and vital signs—no history, vital signs after fluid bolus 90/60, Pulse 110, Respiration 20
  Neurological—unchanged from above
  Head—contusion of forehead, no fluid from nose or ears, no Battle's sign or raccoon eyes, face stable
  Airway—open, gag reflex still present
  Breathing—normal rate and depth
  Neck—no sign of trauma
    Trachea—midline
    Neck veins—flat

Circulation—BP as above, skin now pale, cool, clammy

Chest—no change, heart sounds—normal, but slightly irregular

Abdomen—more distended, patient moans and localizes to palpation

Pelvis—no need to examine again

Extremities

Upper—normal, weak distal pulses, moves to pain

Lower—normal, weak distal pulses, moves to pain

Decision—maintain IV fluids to keep BP in range of about 110 systolic, watch for loss of gag reflex—isn't a noncontrolled bleed BP maintenance of 100 systolic

Ongoing exam

Subjective changes—patient unconscious

Neurological

LOC—unchanged

Pupils—equal and reactive

GSC— (8) eyes—2 , verbal—1, motor—5

Gag reflex no longer present

Airway—open, no gag reflex, needs intubation

Breathing—normal rate and depth

Circulation

Blood pressure—110/70

Pulses—rate 110

Skin color, condition, and temperature—pale, cold, clammy

Neck—unchanged

Trachea—midline

Neck veins—flat

Chest—unchanged, heart sounds—normal, but slightly irregular

Abdomen—distended and tender

Focused assessment of injuries

Sternal fracture unchanged

Intra-abdominal bleeding continues

Blunt head trauma unchanged

Check interventions

Is oxygen hooked up and turned on?

Is patient intubated and the tube in the trachea?

Are IVs running at correct rate?

Cardiac monitor and pulse oximeter applied? Multiple PVCs, 96 percent

SCENARIO 5

Setting

EMS/Prehospital

Police request assistance at the scene of a murder suicide. A male is confirmed dead from a gunshot to the head while a female is lying supine holding her arm.

History

    S—"I can't get my breath. It hurts to breathe. I think my arm is broken."
    A—allergic to tetanus toxoid
    M—none
    P—hemophilia
    L—three hours ago
    E—"I tried to stop him from attacking me and he broke my arm then he shot me!"

Nursing/Medical

Police respond to the scene of a murder suicide. A male is confirmed dead from a gunshot to the head. Neighbors take a female to the nearby hospital before EMS arrives.

History

    S—"I can't get my breath. It hurts to breathe. I think my arm is broken."
    A—allergic to tetanus toxoid
    M—none
    P—hemophilia
    L—three hours ago
    E—"I tried to stop him from attacking me and he broke my arm then he shot me!"

Occupational Health/Industrial

The husband of one of your workers has come to the plant, hit her with a bat and shot her in the chest. He then shot himself in the head.

History

    S—"I can't get my breath. It hurts to breathe. I think my arm is broken."
    A—allergic to tetanus toxoid
    M—none
    P—negative for serious illness
    L—three hours ago
    E—"I tried to stop him from attacking me and he broke my arm then he shot me!"

Military

You are on the front line and are called to rescue a soldier who has been injured by an explosion.

History

       S—"I can't get my breath. It hurts to breathe. I think my arm is broken."

       A—allergic to tetanus toxoid

       M—none

       P—negative for serious illness

       L—three hours ago

       E—"A shell went off nearby and blew me up against this rock wall."

Injuries

1. Sucking chest wound on the right side

2. Fracture of left forearm

3. Hemothorax on right side

4. Shock

Patient Instructions

You are alert but have difficulty breathing and are in great pain. Cry out in pain when anyone touches your left arm.

Moulage Instructions

Sucking chest wound and bruises on arm can be made as described in the chapter on moulage techniques. As an alternative, you can simulate the injuries by placing white tape on the affected areas and writing the injury ("sucking chest wound" and "broken arm") with a felt-tip pen. Simulate shock.

Instructor Information

Scene size-up—EMS/prehospital: The police have secured the scene.
               Nursing/medical: Scene safe
               Industrial: Scene safe
               Military: The patient is behind a rock wall at this time. There are no other patients.

Initial assessment
   General impression—potential for critical injuries
   LOC—alert
   Airway—open
   Breathing—rapid rate, poor air movement
   Ventilation instructions—assist ventilation with oxygen
   Circulation:
      Pulses—present at wrist, rapid rate
   Bleeding—still bleeding from the chest wound
   Skin color, condition, and temperature—cyanotic, cold, clammy
Decision—Rapid trauma survey due to mechanism and exam

Rapid trauma survey
   Head—no injury noted
   Neck—no sign of trauma
      Trachea—midline
      Neck veins—flat

Chest—Looking—sucking chest wound on right side, no paradoxical movement, no bruising

Feeling—there is crepitation on the right side

Listening—sucking chest wound on the right, no breath sounds on the right, heart sounds—normal, but difficult to hear because of the sucking wound

Percussion—dull on right side

Abdomen—soft, nontender

Pelvis—stable and nontender

Extremities

Upper legs—normal

Scan of lower legs and arms—swelling, tenderness, deformity of left forearm

Exam of posterior—normal

Decision—load and go, seal sucking chest wound, 2 IV lines

History (obtain from the patient)

Vital signs—BP90/60, pulse 130, respiration 36, temperature normal

Detailed exam (should be done after transport)

History and vital signs—after fluid bolus, BP 100/60, pulse 120, respiration 36

Neurological

LOC—alert

Pupils—equal and reactive

Sensory—normal

Motor—normal

Head—normal

Airway—open, better movement of air if open wound is sealed

Breathing—labored but improved if wound is sealed

Neck—nontender

Trachea—midline

Neck veins—flat

Circulation—BP and pulse as above, skin cyanotic, cool, clammy

Chest—no breath sounds on right, dull to percussion, heart sounds—normal

Abdomen—soft and nontender

Pelvis—no need to reexamine

Extremities

Upper—unchanged, weak pulses, normal sensory and motor

Lower—unchanged, weak pulses, normal sensory and motor

Ongoing exam

Subjective changes—patient complains of severe chest pain and dyspnea

Neurological

LOC—alert

Pupils—equal and reactive

Sensory—normal

Motor—normal

Airway—open

Breathing—still having dyspnea, rapid, shallow respiration

Circulation

Blood pressure—80/60 in spite of fluid bolus

Pulses—rate 140

Skin color, condition, temperature—pale, cool, clammy

Neck—unchanged

Trachea—midline

Neck veins—flat

Chest—unchanged, heart sounds—normal

Abdomen—soft and nontender

Focused assessment of injuries

    Chest wound sealed, still dull on right

    Patient still short of breath, even with oxygen

    Left arm should be splinted now, still has normal PMS

Check interventions

    Is oxygen hooked up and turned on?

    Chest wound still sealed?

    Are IVs running at the correct rate?

    Chest dressing blood soaked?

    Splint in good position? PMS OK?

    Cardiac monitor applied? Sinus tachycardia

    Pulse oximeter applied? 92 percent saturation

Decision—notify medical direction that the patient has a right hemothorax and is in shock

SCENARIO 6

Settings

EMS/Prehospital

The patient is an 18-year-old female unrestrained driver who was involved in a motor vehicle collision. While traveling at approximately 60 miles per hour/90 kilometers per hour, she went off the road and hit a tree head-on. She is still in the car.

History

     S—"My hip hurts so bad! My chest and stomach hurt, too!"
     A—allergic to penicillin
     M—taking vitamins and Dilantin
     P—history of epilepsy, seven months pregnant
     L—last meal 2 hours ago
     E—"I was driving down the road and woke up like this. Maybe I had another seizure."

Nursing/Medical

The patient is an 18-year-old female unrestrained driver who was involved in a motor vehicle collision. While traveling at approximately 60 miles per hour/90 kilometers per hour, she went off the road and hit a tree head-on. She was moved to another car by friends and transported to your location because they were afraid she might have the baby.

History

     S—"My hip hurts so bad! My chest and stomach hurt, too!"
     A—allergic to penicillin
     M—taking vitamins and Dilantin
     P—history of epilepsy, seven months pregnant
     L—last meal 2 hours ago
     E—"I was driving down the road and woke up when my friends were moving me. Maybe I had another seizure."

Occupational Health/Industrial

The patient is an 18-year-old female employee who was unrestrained in her car. She was exiting the road into the parking lot at the factory at approximately 60 miles per hour/90 kilometers per hour and hit a tree head-on. She is still in the car.

History

     S—"My hip hurts so bad! My chest and stomach hurt, too!"
     A—allergic to penicillin
     M—taking vitamins and Dilantin
     P—history of epilepsy, seven months pregnant
     L—last meal 5 hours ago
     E—"I was driving down the road and woke up like this. Maybe I had another seizure."

Military

An 18-year-old female is the civilian daughter of the general. She was walking to her car after lunch at the officer's club when a truck struck her.

History

>   S—"My hip hurts so bad! My chest and stomach hurt, too!"
>   A—allergic to penicillin
>   M—taking vitamins and Dilantin
>   P—history of epilepsy, seven months pregnant
>   L—last meal in the last hour
>   E—"I was walking to my car and woke up like this. I don't know what happened."

Injuries

1. Posterior dislocation of left hip
2. Fractured pelvis
3. Shock
4. Contusion of sternum

Patient Instructions

You should be alert and complain of pain in the chest, abdomen, and left hip. When examined, you should complain of pain when the sternum or anterior ribs are palpated, when the pelvis is palpated, or when the left leg is moved in any way. Do not allow your left leg to be straightened. Scream at the top of your lungs at any attempt to straighten your left leg. Continually say "I am pregnant; what about my baby?"

Moulage Instructions

Apply bruise to sternum. Use one pillow to simulate pregnancy (unless model is actually pregnant). Simulate diaphoresis.

Instructor Information

Scene size-up—the scene is safe in all settings. Mechanism depends on the setting chosen. No other patients.
Initial assessment
    General impression—potential for serious injuries
    LOC—normal
    Airway—open
    Breathing—normal rate and quality
    Ventilation instructions—give supplemental oxygen
    Circulation:
        Pulses—rapid, present at the wrist
        Bleeding—no external bleeding
        Skin color, condition, and temperature—good color, warm and dry
Decision—Rapid trauma survey due to mechanism
Rapid trauma survey

Head—no obvious injury
Neck—normal, nontender
  Trachea—midline
  Neck veins—flat
Chest—Looking—contusion of sternum
  Feeling—tender sternum, no instability
  Listening—breath sounds present and equal, heart sounds—normal
Abdomen—very pregnant (uterus to the xyphoid), tender
Pelvis—tender, unstable
Extremities
  Upper legs—left leg flexed at the hip and knee, internally rotated, right leg normal
  Scan of lower legs and arms—normal
Exam of posterior—normal
Decision—load and go (fractured pelvis), two IV lines, splint dislocated hip
History (obtain from the patient)
Vital signs—BP 90/60, pulse 140, respiration 24, temperature normal

Detailed exam (should be done after transport)
  History and vital signs—if given a bolus of IV fluids, BP is 100/70, pulse 110, respiration 24
  Neurological
    LOC—alert and oriented
    Pupils—equal and reactive
    Sensory—normal
    Motor—normal
  Head—normal, no fluid from ears or nose
  Airway—open
  Breathing—normal rate and quality
  Neck—no tenderness or sign of trauma
    Trachea—midline
    Neck veins—flat
  Circulation—no external bleeding, skin pale, cool, diaphoretic
  Chest—Looking—unchanged
        Feeling—sternal and anterior rib tenderness
        Listening—breath sounds still present and equal, heart sounds—normal
  Abdomen—more tender
  Pelvis—do not examine again
  Extremities
    Upper—normal
    Lower—unchanged from above, weak distal pulses, normal sensation, you cannot straighten
      left hip

Ongoing exam
  Subjective changes—patient complains of increasing abdominal pain
  Neurological
    LOC—alert
    Pupils—equal and reactive
    Sensory—normal
    Motor—normal
  Airway—open
  Breathing—normal

Circulation
    Blood pressure—if no IV fluids: BP 60/40, if IV fluids: BP 100/60
    Pulses—rate if no IV fluids: 160, if IV fluids: 110
    Skin color, condition, and temperature—pale, cool, clammy
Neck—no change
    Trachea—midline
    Neck veins—flat
Chest—unchanged, heart sounds—normal
Abdomen—very tender
Focused assessment of injuries
    Contusion of sternum—monitoring heart
    Posterior dislocation of hip—splinted
    Fractured pelvis—stabilized on spine board
    Shock—fluid boluses
Check interventions
    Is oxygen hooked up and turned on?
    Hip splinted in flexed position?
    Are IVs running at correct rate?
    Patient on backboard tilted to the left?
    Cardiac monitor—sinus tachycardia
    Pulse oximeter—100 percent

SCENARIO 7

Setting

EMS/Prehospital

A 30-year-old male involved with road construction falls into a rock-crushing machine. Co-workers stop the machine, pull him out and lay him on the side of the road.

History

S—patient unresponsive

A—none

M—none

P—diabetic

L—last meal was four hours ago

E—"The supervisor saw him fall in and yelled for someone to stop the machine but he was already badly hurt!"

Nursing/Medical

A 30-year-old male involved with road construction falls into a rock-crushing machine. Co-workers stop the machine, pull him out, and transport him in the box of a dump truck to your facility.

History

S—patient unresponsive

A—none

M—none

P—diabetic

L—last meal was four hours ago

E—"The supervisor saw him fall in and yelled for someone to stop the machine but he was already badly hurt!"

Occupational Health/Industrial

A 30-year-old male involved with road construction falls into a rock-crushing machine. Co-workers stop the machine, pull him out and lay him on the side of the road.

History

S—patient unresponsive

A—none

M—none

P—diabetic

L—last meal was four hours ago

E—"The supervisor saw him fall in and yelled for someone to stop the machine but he was already badly hurt!"

Military

Soldiers were involved in mine sweeping operations when a mine exploded leaving one soldier badly injured and another with skin abrasions.

History

Not available.

Injuries

1. Basilar skull fracture on the right side
2. Both legs crushed and mangled
3. Fractured pelvis
4. Large laceration of abdomen with protruding viscera

PATIENT INSTRUCTIONS

The patient remains unresponsive.

Moulage Instructions

You may use a live model, but any mannequin, including a Resusci-Annie™, can be used. The protruding viscera can best be simulated with commercial strap-on moulage, but it can be made (see makeup techniques). Bleeding from the legs can best be simulated with red paper or cloth on which "active bleeding" is written with a felt-tip pen. The closed fracture of the skull can best be made by moulaging a Battle's sign behind the right ear. Put some glycerin or artificial blood in the right ear to represent spinal fluid or blood draining from the ear.

Instructor Information

Scene size-up—the scene is now safe in all settings except the military setting, in which you must be concerned about stepping on another mine. There are no other patients.
Initial assessment
  General impression—critical situation
  LOC—localizes to pain
  Airway—open
  Breathing—normal depth of respiration, the rate seems slow
  Ventilation instructions—should give 100 percent oxygen and assist ventilation at a rate of 12–15 breaths per minute
  Circulation:
    Pulses—present at the neck but not at the wrist, rate rapid
    Bleeding—from both legs and abdominal wound
    Skin color, condition, and temperature—pale, cold, clammy
Decision—rapid trauma survey due to mechanism and exam
Rapid trauma survey
  Head—bruising to right side of face, bloody fluid from right ear

Neck—no obvious trauma
   Trachea—midline
   Neck veins—flat
Chest—Looking—no obvious injury
   Feeling—no TIC
   Listening—breath sounds present and equal bilaterally, heart sounds—normal
Abdomen—protruding viscera, bleeding
Pelvis—very unstable
Extremities
   Upper legs—both legs crushed and mangled from the upper thighs down to the feet, there is
      continued bleeding from both legs
   Scan of lower legs and arms—arms no apparent injuries, legs as above
Exam of posterior—abrasions on lower back
Decision—load and go, cover protruding viscera, pressure dressing to stop bleeding from legs,
   two IV lines, monitor for need to intubate, check fingerstick glucose (120)
History (unobtainable)
Vital signs—BP 50/0, pulse 160, respiration slow when not assisting, temperature normal
Neurological
   LOC—localizes to pain
   Pupils—right dilated and nonreactive, left midposition and reactive
   Sensory—localizes pain
   Motor—moves arms well, little movement in legs
   GSC—(8) eyes—opens to pain (2), verbal—none (1), motor: localizes (5)

Detailed exam (should be done after transport)
   History and vital signs—after fluid bolus: BP 70/50, pulse 130, respiration still slow when not
      assisting
   Neurological
      LOC—localizes to pain
      Pupils—right dilated and nonreactive, left midposition and reactive
      Sensory—localizes pain
      Motor—moves arms well, little movement in legs
      GSC—(8) eyes—opens to pain (2), verbal—none (1), motor: localizes (5)
   Head—Battle's sign behind right ear, bloody fluid from right ear, face stable, no drainage from
      the nose
   Airway—open, no gag reflex, should be intubated
   Breathing—slow and deep when not assisted
   Neck—unchanged
      Trachea—midline
      Neck veins—flat
   Circulation
      BP—90/60 if fluids going, 50/0 if not
      Pulse—130 if fluids going, 160 if not
      Skin color, condition, temperature—pale, cool, clammy
   Chest—unchanged, heart sounds still easily heard
   Abdomen—bleeding controlled with dressings
   Pelvis—do not examine again
   Extremities
      Upper—normal

Lower—continue to bleed unless tourniquets applied
Decision—tourniquets to legs, give fluids to get BP to 110 systolic, intubate

Ongoing exam
   Subjective changes—patient unconscious
   Neurological
      LOC—unchanged
      Pupils—unchanged
      Motor and sensory—unchanged
      GSC—(8) eyes (2), verbal (1), motor (5)
   Airway—should be intubated
   Breathing—should be assisted at 12–15 breaths per minute
   Circulation
      Blood pressure—110/70
      Pulses—rate 130
      Skin color, condition, and temperature—pale, cool, clammy
   Neck—unchanged
      Trachea—midline
      Neck veins—flat
   Chest—unchanged, heart sounds still easily heard
   Abdomen—unchanged
   Focused assessment of injuries
      Basilar skull fracture—still some drainage from the ear, still only localizes to pain, pupils
         unchanged
      Abdomen—no further bleeding if properly dressed
      Pelvis—no further exam
      Legs—bleeding stopped by tourniquets, unable to splint due to extent of the injuries
   Check Interventions
      Is oxygen hooked up and turned on?
      ET tube in the trachea?
      Ventilation rate correct?
      Are IVs running at the correct rate?
      Dressings blood soaked?
      Tourniquets still are controlling the bleeding?
      Cardiac monitor applied?
      Pulse oximeter applied? 98 percent saturation

SCENARIO 8

Settings

EMS/Prehospital

Two teenagers were riding a 4-wheeled all-terrain vehicle. The driver was a 16-year-old female who drove a 4-wheeler into a tree. The driver was killed instantly. The passenger, a 14-year-old male, was thrown into a ditch. Upon arrival, it is obvious that the driver is deceased. The 14-year-old is crying.

Nursing/Medical

Two teenagers were riding a 4-wheeled all-terrain vehicle. The driver was a 16-year-old female who drove the 4-wheeler into a tree. The passenger, a 14-year-old male, was thrown into a ditch. A BLS ambulance has just arrived at your facility with both patients without prior notification. Upon arrival, it is obvious that the 16-year-old is deceased. The 14-year old is crying and is poorly strapped to a spine board.

Occupational Health/Industrial

Two teenagers were riding a 4-wheeled all-terrain vehicle. The driver was a 16-year-old female who drove the 4-wheeler into a tree. The driver was killed instantly. The passenger, a 14-year-old male, was thrown into a ditch. Your clinic is close to the collision so you take a medical kit and go to the scene. Upon arrival, it is obvious that the 16-year-old is deceased. The 14-year-old is crying.

Military

Two teenagers were riding a 4-wheeled all-terrain vehicle on the military base. The driver was a 16-year-old female who drove the 4-wheeler into a tree. The driver was killed instantly. The passenger, a 14-year-old male, was thrown into a ditch. You are a medic on the military ambulance. Upon arrival, it is obvious that the driver is deceased. The 14-year-old is crying.

History

> S—"My leg is killing me! Please help!"
> A—no allergies
> M—no medications
> P—no significant past illnesses
> L—last meal two hours ago
> E—"I was on the back with my sister and we hit a tree. How is she doing? I want her here with me!!!"

Injuries

1. Open fracture of the right lower leg
2. Fracture of pelvis
3. Shock

Patient Instructions

You should be alert and complain of pain in the right lower leg. When your pelvis is examined, you should cry out loudly with pain.

Moulage Instructions

Full-face or half-face helmet should be in place in all settings. Open fracture is best done with commercial strap-on moulage but can be made with wax or plumber's putty and pieces of bone. Simulate diaphoresis.

Instructor Information

Scene size-up—scene safe, other patient deceased
Initial assessment
   General impression—potential for critical injuries
   LOC—alert
   Airway—open (helmet must be removed to evaluate)
   Breathing—rate and quality normal
   Ventilation instructions—may give oxygen
   Circulation:
      Pulses—present at the wrist, rate seems increased
      Bleeding—slight bleeding from right lower leg
      Skin color, condition, and temperature—warm and dry, color normal
Decision—rapid trauma survey due to mechanism
Rapid trauma survey
   Head—no sign of trauma (was wearing helmet)
   Neck—normal
      Trachea—midline
      Neck veins—flat
   Chest—Looking—no DCAPP-BTLS
         Feeling—no TIC
         Listening—breath sounds present and equal, normal heart sounds
   Abdomen—slight tenderness of lower abdomen
   Pelvis—unstable and tender
   Extremities
      Upper legs—normal
      Scan of lower legs and arms—open fracture of right lower leg, arms normal
   Exam of posterior—normal
   Decision—load and go (unstable pelvis), two IV lines, splint leg
   History (obtain from the patient)
   Vital signs—BP 90/70, pulse 160, respiration 32, temperature normal

Detailed exam (should be done after transport)
   History and vital signs—BP 90/70, pulse 160, respiration 32,
   Neurological
      LOC—alert
      Pupils—equal and reactive
      Sensory—normal
      Motor—normal

Head—normal
Airway—open
Breathing—normal rate and quality
Neck—nontender
    Trachea—midline
    Neck veins—flat
Circulation—BP and pulse as above, skin: pale, cool, clammy
Chest—unchanged, normal heart sounds
Abdomen—no change
Pelvis—do not examine again
Extremities
    Upper—normal, good PMS
    Lower—open fracture of right lower leg, distal pulses palpable, normal sensory, can wiggle
       toes, no bleeding if dressed
Decision—record and continue to monitor

Ongoing exam
    Subjective changes—abdominal pain is worse
    Neurological
        LOC—normal
        Pupils—equal and reactive
        Sensory and motor—normal
    Airway—open
    Breathing—normal rate and quality
    Circulation
        Blood pressure—80/50
        Pulses—rate 175
        Skin color, condition, and temperature—pale, cool, clammy
    Neck—nontender
        Trachea—midline
        Neck veins—flat
    Chest—unchanged, normal heart sounds
    Abdomen—more tender in lower abdomen
    Focused assessment of injuries
        Leg—splinted, still has good PMS, no bleeding now
        Pelvis—not rechecked
        Abdomen—still tender
    Check interventions
        Is oxygen hooked up and turned on?
        Dressing blood soaked?
        Are IVs running at correct rate to maintain BP of at least 90?
        Splint in good position?
    Decision—continue present treatment

SCENARIO 9

Setting

EMS/Prehospital

The patient is a young male who was riding his horse when he was knocked from the horse by a low tree branch. He subsequently fell down a steep cliff. His riding companion called for help.

History

> S—"I hurt all over."
> A—allergic to penicillin
> M—insulin
> P—diabetes
> L—last meal was last night, approximately 18 hours ago
> E—"I was going home and my horse started galloping out of control, then I hit a branch that knocked me off and fell down the cliff."

Nursing/Medical

The patient is a young male who was riding his horse when he was knocked from the horse by a low tree branch. He subsequently fell down a steep cliff. His riding companion called for help and a nearby farmer put him in the back of his pickup truck and drove to your facility.

History

> S—"I hurt all over."
> A—allergic to penicillin
> M—insulin
> P—diabetes
> L—last meal was last night, approximately 18 hours ago
> E—"I was going home and my horse started galloping out of control, then I hit a branch that knocked me off and fell down the cliff."

Occupational Health/Industrial

One of your truck drivers runs head-on into the brick company sign without slowing down. He tried to get away from the vehicle but collapsed after one step.

History

> S—"I hurt all over."
> A—allergic to penicillin
> M—insulin
> P—diabetes
> L—last meal was last night. Did not eat breakfast this morning.
> E—"I swerved to miss an animal and ran into a sign."

Military

The patient is a teen-age dependent of one of the officers on your base. He falls from a third-floor balcony onto concrete.

History

> S—"I hurt all over."
> A—allergic to penicillin
> M—insulin
> P—diabetes
> L—last meal was last night. Did not eat breakfast.
> E—"I don't remember."

Injuries

1. Intraabdominal bleeding
2. Fracture of left femur
3. Scalp laceration
4. Hypoglycemia (when asked, fingerstick glucose is 40)

Patient Instructions

Complain of pain when your abdomen is palpated or your left upper leg is examined.

Moulage Instructions

Use trousers with a large tear in left thigh area. The left thigh should have a large bruise. Apply some fake blood to an area of the scalp (fake blood mixed with KY jelly works well here). Don't use this on someone with light-colored hair, as it will stain the hair.

Instructor Information

Scene size-up—no danger, no other patients
Initial Assessment
   General impression—potential for critical injuries
   LOC—alert but confused
   Airway—open
   Breathing—normal rate and quality
   Ventilation instructions—apply oxygen, assist if needed
   Circulation:
       Pulses—present at neck and wrist, rate seems fast
       Bleeding—some bleeding from the scalp wound
       Skin color, condition and temperature—normal
Decision—rapid trauma survey due to mechanism
Rapid trauma survey
   Head—bleeding from scalp laceration, otherwise normal
   Neck—no swelling or discoloration
       Trachea—midline

Neck veins—flat
Chest—Looking—normal
        Feeling—no TIC
        Listening—breath sounds present and equal, normal heart sounds
Abdomen—diffusely tender to palpation
Pelvis—stable and nontender
Extremities
    Upper legs—swelling, tenderness, and deformity of left upper leg
    Scan of lower legs and arms—normal
Exam of posterior—normal
Decision—load and go, two IV lines, traction splint left femur, blood glucose (40).
    Give IV glucose
History (obtain from the patient)
Vital sign—BP 110/70, pulse 100, respiration 22, temperature normal
Neurological
    LOC—awake but confused
    Pupils—equal and reactive
    Sensory—normal
    Motor—normal
    GSC—(14) eyes (4), verbal (3), motor (6)

Detailed exam (should be done after transport)
   History and vital signs—as above
   Neurological
      LOC—alert and oriented if given glucose, awake but confused if not
      Pupils—equal and reactive
      Sensory—normal
      Motor—normal
   Head—blood in hair from scalp laceration, no Battle's sign or raccoon eyes, face normal
   Airway—open
   Breathing—normal rate and depth
   Neck—nontender
      Trachea—midline
      Neck veins—flat
   Circulation—BP and pulse as above, skin warm and dry but pale
   Chest—no change, normal heart sounds
   Abdomen—more tender
   Pelvis—do not examine again
   Extremities
      Upper—normal
      Lower—left leg should be splinted, good PMS
   Decision—give IV glucose if not already done

Ongoing exam
   Subjective changes—abdominal pain is worse
   Neurological
      LOC—alert and oriented if given glucose, decrease LOC if no glucose given
      Pupils—equal and reactive
      Sensory and motor—unchanged
   Airway—open

Breathing—normal rate and quality
Circulation
    Blood pressure—60/40
    Pulses—rate 150
    Skin color, condition, and temperature—pale, cool, clammy
Neck—nontender
    Trachea—midline
    Neck veins—flat
Chest—normal, heart sounds—normal
Abdomen—distended and tender
Focused assessment of injuries
    Abdomen—worsening
    Scalp—no longer bleeding if dressed
    Left leg—unchanged
    Hypoglycemia—recheck glucose (136)
Check interventions
    Is oxygen hooked up and turned on?
    Blood glucose rechecked? (136)
    Are IVs running at correct rate to maintain systolic BP of 90–100?
    Dressing blood soaked?
    Splint in good position?
    Cardiac monitor applied?
    Pulse oximeter applied? 98 percent saturation
Decision—fluid bolus

SCENARIO 10

Setting

EMS/Prehospital

A male motorcyclist looses control on a curve and collides with a guardrail. Police call for medical assistance when they determine the man is injured and unable to move.

History

S—"I can't feel anything. I can't move."
A—none
M—none
P—good health
L—6 hours ago
E—"I tried to lay the motorcycle down when I lost control but the guardrail caught me."

Nursing/Medical

A male motorcyclist looses control on a curve and collides with a guardrail. Police call for medical assistance when they determine the man is injured and unable to move, but EMS is significantly delayed so they transport the patient to the hospital in the back of a police van.

History

S—"I can't feel anything. I can't move."
A—none
M—none
P—good health
L—6 hours ago
E—"I tried to lay the motorcycle down when I lost control but the guardrail caught me."

Occupational Health/Industrial

A male crane operator slips and falls (30 feet/10 meters) while climbing down the crane for lunch. A co-worker witnesses the fall and notifies you.

History

S—"I can't feel anything. I can't move."
A—none
M—none
P—good health
L—6 hours ago
E—"I was climbing down the crane for lunch like I do every day but somehow slipped ."

Military

A male recruit is repelling unsupervised from a platform when he looses his grip and falls 30 feet/10 meters. The drill sergeant finds the recruit and notifies you.

History

    S—"I can't feel anything. I can't move."
    A—none
    M—none
    P—good health
    L—6 hours ago
    E—"I was practicing climbing so I could pass the test."

Injuries

1. Fractured lower neck with spinal cord injury
2. Spinal shock
3. Fractured right tibia (open)

Patient Instructions

Complain of pain when your neck is examined. You can flex your arms at the elbows but have weak grip with your hands; otherwise you are unable to move.

Moulage Instructions

The patient should wear a full-face motorcycle helmet. A partial-face helmet is an alternative. For OH/industry and military, have patient wear a hard hat or military helmet.

Instructor Information

Scene size-up—safe, no other patients
Initial assessment
    General impression—possible neck and spinal injury
    LOC—alert
    Airway—open
    Breathing—normal rate, shallow, diaphragmatic only
    Ventilation instructions—assist ventilation with oxygen
    Circulation:
        Pulses—present at wrist, rapid (still has catecholamines present)
        Bleeding—none
        Skin color, condition, and temperature—normal color, sweaty, warm
Decision—rapid trauma survey due to mechanism and exam
Rapid trauma survey
    Head—face normal, helmet still in place
    Neck—tenderness at base of neck
        Trachea—midline
        Neck veins—flat
    Chest—Looking—no movement of ribs with breathing, otherwise normal

Feeling—no TIC, no sensation
Listening—breath sounds present and equal, heart sounds—normal
Abdomen—soft, no sensation
Pelvis—stable
Extremities
Upper legs—normal
Scan of lower legs and arms—right tibia protruding, can flex arms, weak grips bilaterally, pulses present
Exam of posterior—normal
Decision—spinal injury, load and go
History (obtain from the patient)
Vital signs—BP 70/50, pulse 70, respiration 18, temperature normal

Detailed Exam (should be done after transport)
History and vital signs—after fluid challenge BP 80/60
Neurological
LOC—alert and oriented
Pupils—equal and reactive
Sensory—no sensation from the neck down
Motor—can flex arms, weak grips bilaterally, no movement below the shoulders
Head—face normal, helmet still in place
Airway—open
Breathing—rate 18, shallow
Neck—still tender, some swelling
Trachea—midline
Neck veins—flat
Circulation—BP and pulse as above, skin warm and dry
Chest—unchanged, heart sounds– unchanged
Abdomen—unchanged
Pelvis—do not examine again
Extremities
Upper—unchanged
Lower—unchanged

Ongoing exam
Subjective changes—patient still has no feeling from the neck down
Neurological
LOC—normal
Pupils—equal and reactive
Sensory and motor—unchanged
Airway—open
Breathing—unchanged
Circulation
Blood pressure—80/60 if fluids given
Pulses—rate 70
Skin color, condition, and temperature—warm, dry, pink
Neck—unchanged
Trachea—unchanged
Neck veins—unchanged

Chest—unchanged, heart sounds—normal
Abdomen—unchanged
Focused assessment of injuries
No change in neurological exam
Check interventions
Is oxygen hooked up and turned on?
Assisting respiration?
Are IVs running at correct rate?
Helmet left in place?
Splint?

SCENARIO 11

Settings

EMS/Prehospital

The patient is a 50-year-old male semitruck driver who collided with a train at an uncontrolled crossing. He was ejected from the truck and is lying in the ditch.

Medical/Nursing

The patient is a 50-year-old male semitruck driver who collided with a train at an uncontrolled crossing. He was ejected from the truck and transported by community first responders to your location.

Occupational Health/Industrial

The patient is a 50-year-old male semitruck driver who collided with a train at an uncontrolled crossing just outside the gate to your plant. He was ejected from the truck and is lying in the ditch.

Military

The patient is a 50-year-old male supply clerk who was driving a 6 × 6 truck and collided with a train at an uncontrolled crossing. He was ejected from the 6 × 6 and is lying in the ditch.

History

Not available

Injuries

1. Fractured left femur (closed)
2. Fractured pelvis
3. Fractured ribs on left side with flail section
4. Shock
5. Closed head injury

Patient Instructions

Unconscious with no response to stimulus.

Moulage Instructions

Create bruising over ribs. Create bruising and swelling over femur. Simulate cyanosis and diaphoresis.

Instructor Information

Scene size-up—the scene is safe in all settings. Mechanism depends on the setting chosen. No other patients.
Initial assessment
    General impression—potential for serious injuries
    LOC—curses and localizes to pain

Airway—open
Breathing—normal quality, increased rate
Ventilation instructions—give supplemental oxygen
Circulation:
    Pulses—rapid, present at the wrist
    Bleeding—no external bleeding
    Skin color, condition, and temperature—pale, clammy and cool
Decision—rapid trauma survey due to mechanism
Rapid trauma survey
    Head—no obvious injury
    Neck—normal, nontender
        Trachea—midline
        Neck veins—flat
    Chest—Looking—bruising over left chest
            Feeling—unstable section of anterior ribs on left side
            Listening—breath sounds present and equal, heart sounds—normal
    Abdomen—normal
    Pelvis—unstable
    Extremities
        Upper legs—left leg swollen and bruised midfemur, right leg normal
        Scan of lower legs and arms—normal
    Exam of posterior—normal
    Decision—load and go (fractured pelvis), two IV lines, splint fractured femur
    History—unable to obtain because of patient's level of consciousness
    Vital signs—BP 80/60, pulse 140, respiration 24, temperature normal
    GCS—eyes: open to pain (2), verbal: curses to pain (3), motor: localizes to pain (5)

Detailed exam (should be done after transport)
    History and vital signs—if given a bolus of IV fluids BP is 90/70, pulse 120, respiration 24
    Neurological
        LOC—curses to pain
        Pupils—equal and reactive
        Sensory—localizes to pain
        Motor—moves all extremities
        GCS—unchanged
        Blood glucose—138
    Head—normal, no fluid from ears or nose
    Airway—open
    Breathing—normal rate and quality
    Neck—no tenderness or sign of trauma
        Trachea—midline
        Neck veins—flat
    Circulation—no external bleeding, skin pale, cool, diaphoretic
    Chest—Looking—unchanged
            Feeling—anterior rib instability
            Listening—breath sounds still present and equal, heart sounds—normal
    Abdomen—no change
    Pelvis—do not examine again
    Extremities
        Upper—normal

Lower—unchanged from above, weak distal pulses

Ongoing exam
   Neurological
      LOC—curses to pain
      Pupils—equal and reactive
      Sensory—localizes to pain
      Motor—moves all extremities
      GCS—unchanged
   Airway—open
   Breathing—normal
   Circulation
      Blood pressure—if no IV fluids: BP 60/40, if IV fluids: BP 90/70
      Pulses—rate if no IV fluids: 160, if IV fluids: 110
      Skin color, condition, and temperature—pale, cool, clammy
   Neck—no change
      Trachea—midline
      Neck veins—flat
   Chest—unchanged, heart sounds—normal
   Abdomen—very tender
   Focused assessment of injuries
      Rib fractures—check flail and monitor heart
      Fractured femur—traction splint
      Fractured pelvis—stabilized on spine board
      Shock—fluid boluses
   Check interventions
      Is oxygen hooked up and turned on?
      Are IVs running at correct rate to maintain BP of 110–120 systolic?
      Controlled flail segment?
      Cardiac monitor—sinus tachycardia
      Pulse oximeter—100 percent

SCENARIO 12

Setting

EMS/Prehospital

A young male at a building site was struck by a collapsing wall and debris. The man is under some rubble; however, you have full, easy access to him. Scene appears safe.

Nursing/Medical

A young male at a building demolition site was struck by a collapsing wall and debris. His co-workers put him in the back of their pickup and brought him to your emergency department. The attending physician is with a cardiac arrest and cannot immediately assist you.

Occupational Health/Industrial

A young male at a building demolition site was struck by a collapsing wall and debris. The man is under some rubble; however, you have full, easy access to him. Scene appears safe.

Military

The patient is a young soldier who was on a "clearing mission" when a booby trap was tripped causing a structural cave-in.

History

S—Pain in chest and right lower leg, "tingling all over," difficulty breathing and ringing in his ears
A—no allergies
M—no medications
P—no significant past illnesses
L—last meal three hours ago
E—"All I saw was a something falling on me!"

Injuries

1. Open fracture of the right lower leg
2. Cervical spine injury
3. Flail chest on the right side
4. Fracture of pelvis
5. Shock

Patient Instructions

You should be alert and complain of pain in the chest and right lower leg. You should describe "tingling all over" and complain of difficulty breathing and ringing in his ears and it is hard to hear. When your pelvis is examined, you should cry out loudly with pain.

Moulage Instructions

Open fracture is best done with commercial strap-on moulage but can be made with wax or plumber's putty and pieces of bone (see makeup techniques in the appendix). The strap-on moulage is not as realistic but holds up much better during a long day of use. Flail chest is best made by applying a piece of white tape to the chest and, using a felt-tip pen, writing "flail chest" on it. Dirt around mouth, nose, and eyes.

Instructor Information

Scene size-up—no danger, mechanism of injury is as described, no other patients
Initial assessment
    General impression—does not appear critically injured initially
    LOC—alert and responds appropriately
    Airway—open and clear
    Breathing—rate increased, quality labored
    Ventilation instructions—should order 100% oxygen
    Circulation:
        Pulses—present and strong at the wrist, rate seems increased
        Bleeding—no external bleeding noted other than some blood on right lower leg (not actively
          bleeding)
        Skin color, condition, and temperature—warm and dry but slightly cyanotic
Decision—do rapid trauma survey due to mechanism
Rapid Trauma Survey
    Head—minor bruising and small abrasions on face and neck
    Neck—no discoloration or swelling, tender to palpation
        Trachea—midline
        Neck veins—flat
    Chest—Looking—paradoxical motion of right chest
        Feeling—instability and crepitation right chest
        Listening—breath sounds decreased on right, heart sounds- normal
        Percussion—equal
    Abdomen—soft, slightly tender in lower quadrants
    Pelvis—unstable, painful to palpation
    Extremities
        Upper legs—no apparent injury
        Scan of lower legs and arms—open fracture of right lower leg, no active bleeding, normal PMS
    Exam of posterior—normal except that the neck is tender
    Decision—load and go due to flail chest and respiratory difficulty, notify medical direction, two
        IV lines, stabilize flail segment, 100 percent oxygen
    History (obtain from the patient)
    Vital signs—BP 120/90, pulse 110, respiration 30 and labored, temperature feels normal

Detailed exam (should be done after transport)
    History and vital signs—unchanged from above
    Neurological
        LOC—responds to verbal stimuli but now is pale and lethargic
        Pupils—equal and reactive
        Sensory—abnormal "tingling" sensation below the neck
        Motor—normal

GCS—(14), eyes (4), verbal (4), motor (6)

Head—scalp normal, negative Battle's sign and raccoon eyes, no fluid from ears or nose, face stable

Airway—open and clear

Breathing—still labored with rate of 30/min

Neck—tender to palpationt

    Trachea—midline

    Neck veins—flat

Circulation—skin now pale, cool, and diaphoretic, repeat BP is 80/50

Chest—Looking—flail should be stabilized

        Feeling—no change

        Listening—still has decreased breath sounds on right side, heart sounds—normal

        Percussion—still equal

Abdomen—slight tenderness in lower quadrants, not distended

Pelvis—already examined; do not examine again

Extremities

    Upper—minor scrapes and abrasions

    Lower—should have splint and dressing on fracture of right lower leg, PMS is unchanged

Decision—check that the patient is getting 100 percent oxygen, give fluid bolus, check fingerstick glucose—120

Ongoing exam

    Subjective changes—patient feels better now

    Neurological

        LOC—more alert after fluid bolus

        Pupils—equal and reactive

        GCS—(15), eyes—4, verbal—5, motor—6

    Airway—clear and open

    Breathing—still painful with rate of 30/min but moving air better with stabilization of the flail

    Circulation

        Blood pressure—90/50

        Pulses—rate 130

        Skin color, condition, temperature—still pale, cool, diaphoretic

    Neck—unchanged

        Trachea—still midline

        Neck veins—still flat

    Chest—unchanged, heart sounds—normal

    Abdomen—unchanged

    Focused assessment of injuries

        Neck stabilized?

        Flail chest stabilized?

        Open fracture dressed and splinted? No bleeding

        Shock being managed with cautious fluid resuscitation?

    Check interventions

        Is oxygen hooked up and turned on?

        Is flail chest still stabilized?

        Are IVs running at a rate to maintain BP of 90–100 systolic?

        Is fracture well splinted and wound dressed?

        Cardiac monitor applied?

        Pulse oximeter applied? 92 percent saturation

SCENARIO 13

Settings

EMS/Prehospital

A park employee was mowing grass on the side of a road when his tractor was struck on the left rear side by a truck traveling at high speed. The operator of the tractor was thrown from his tractor approximately 18 meters/16 yards.

Nursing/Medical

A park employee was mowing grass on the side of a road when his tractor was struck on the left rear side by a truck traveling at high speed. The operator of the tractor was thrown from his tractor approximately 18 meters/16 yards. Local first responders brought him to your emergency department. Your attending physician is with a cardiac arrest and cannot immediately respond.

Occupational Health/Industrial

A company grounds employee was mowing grass on the side of a road when his tractor was struck on the left rear side by a truck traveling at high speed. The operator of the tractor was thrown from his tractor approximately 18 meters/16 yards.

Military

A PFC was mowing grass on the side of the protected area of the installation when his tractor was struck on the left rear side by a truck traveling at high speed. The operator of the tractor was thrown from his tractor approximately 18 meters/16 yards.

History

> S—"My chest & hips are killing me!"
> A—none
> M—"I take blood pressure pills and allergy pills" (for military scenario—no medications)
> P—high blood pressure (for military scenario—no significant past history)
> L—last meal 3 hours ago
> E—"I don't know where that truck came from that hit me!"

Injuries

1. Fracture of C-7, but the spinal cord has not been injured yet
2. Flail chest on the left
3. Ruptured spleen
4. Multiple fractures of the pelvis

Patient Instructions

You are awake and alert. Complain of pain in the left chest and hip. Do not complain of abdominal or neck pain. When the neck and abdomen are checked, complain of tenderness. When pelvis is checked, complain of severe pain. Complain of difficulty breathing when your chest is examined.

Moulage Instructions

Place white tape on left side of chest. Label "flail chest" with a felt-tip pen.

Instructor Information

Scene size-up—the scene is safe
Initial assessment
    General impression—potential for critical injuries
    LOC—alert and oriented
    Airway—open and clear
    Breathing—rapid, shallow, labored respiration
    Ventilation instructions—supplemental oxygen, assist ventilation as needed. Intubate if respiration worsens.
    Circulation:
        Pulses—rapid, present at the wrist
        Bleeding—no external bleeding noted
        Skin color, condition and temperature—cyanotic, pale, diaphoretic
Decision—rapid trauma survey based on mechanism and initial assessment
Rapid trauma survey
    Head—no injuries noted
    Neck—tender to palpation
        Trachea—midline
        Neck veins—flat
    Chest—Looking—paradoxical movement on the left side
            Feeling—unstable segment on the left
            Listening—breath sounds decreased on the left, good heart sounds
            Percussion—equal bilaterally
    Abdomen—slightly tender to palpation
    Pelvis—unstable and tender
    Extremities
        Upper legs—no sign of injury
        Scan of lower legs and arms—no sign of injury
    Exam of posterior—no injury noted
    Decision—load and go, stabilize flail segment, two IV lines, monitor for shock
    History (obtain from the patient)
    Vital signs—BP 90/60, pulse 130, respiration 36, temperature normal

Detailed exam (should be done after transport)
    History and vital signs—after fluid bolus: BP 100/60, pulse 120, respiration 30 and less painful if flail segment stabilized
    Neurological
        LOC—alert
        Pupils—equal and reactive
        Sensory—normal
        Motor—normal
    Head—scalp normal, no drainage from ears or nose, negative Battle's sign and raccoon eyes, face stable
    Airway—open
    Breathing—rate and quality improved if flail has been stabilized

Neck—some swelling now, more tendert
    Trachea—midline
    Neck veins—flat
Circulation
    BP as above
    Pulse as above
    Skin color, condition, and temperature—pale, cool, clammy
Chest—Looking—should have flail segment stabilized
        Feeling—should not palpate again
        Listening—decreased breath sounds on left, heart sounds unchanged
        Percussion—still equal
Abdomen—distended and painful now
Pelvis—should not be examined again
Extremities
    Upper—no DCAP-BTLS, good PMS
    Lower—no DCAP-BTLS, good PMS
Decision—continue present therapy, monitor for need to intubate

Ongoing exam
    Subjective changes—patient complains of worsening abdominal pain and severe pain with
    breathing
    Neurological
        LOC—normal
        Pupils—equal and reactive
        Sensory and motor—normal
    Airway—open
    Breathing—painful but adequate
    Circulation
        Blood pressure—90/60
        Pulses—rate 130
        Skin color, condition, and temperature—pale, cool, clammy
    Neck—swelling and painful (do not palpate any more)
        Trachea—midline
        Neck veins—flat
    Chest—unchanged, heart sounds—normal
    Abdomen—more distended and tender
    Focused assessment of injuries
        Neck—swollen and tender but no paralysis or weakness
        Flail segment—stabilized, patient splinting on left but no hemothorax
        Abdomen—becoming more tender and distended
    Check interventions
        Is oxygen hooked up and turned on?
        Assisted ventilation as needed?
        Are IVs running at rate to maintain BP of 90–100?
        Flail segment well stabilized? Cardiac monitor applied?
        Pulse oximeter applied? 92 percent saturation

BTLS INTERNATIONAL
BASIC AND ADVANCED PATIENT ASSESSMENT GRADESHEET

Name_____ Student Level_____
Date_____ Scenario #_____ Practice   Test   Retest (circle one)
Times: Start time_____ Transport time_____ Total time_____

Critical Actions   **Notes**
___ Completes scene size-up and uses universal precautions
___ Performs initial assessment and interacts with patient
___ Performs organized rapid trauma survey or focused exam
___ Ensures spinal motion restriction
___ Ensures appropriate oxygenation and ventilation
___ Recognizes and treats all life-threatening injuries
___ Uses appropriate equipment and techniques
___ Recognizes critical trauma, time and transport priorities
___ Performs detailed exam (when time permits)

Important Actions
___ Performs ongoing exam (when time permits)
___ Utilizes time efficiently
___ Gives appropriate report to medical direction
___ Demonstrates acceptable skill techniques
___ Displays leadership and teamwork

Specific Scenario Requirements
___
___
___
___
___

Overall Rating
Excellent:_____ Good:_____ Adequate:_____ Inadequate:_____

Comments

Evaluator's Name _____ Signature _____
Evaluator's Name _____ Signature _____

BTLS INTERNATIONAL SCENARIO GRADE SHEET

Student Name:		Scenario #:	Date:	[ ] Practice [ ] Test [ ] RT
Time Started:	Time Completed Primary:		Time Transported:	Completed Detailed:

ACTION	✓	COMMENTS
ASSESSMENT - PRIMARY SURVEY		
Survey Scene Protective Gear		
Danger		
Number of patients		
More help needed ?		
Mechanism of injury		
LOC Talks to patient		
A.V.P.U.		
Airway		
Breathing rate & quality		
Give appropriate ventilation instructions		
Circulation Pulse at wrist and neck		
Skin color, condition and temp.		
Control major bleeding		
Head Obvious major injury head/face		
Neck Obvious injury		
Trachea		
Neck Veins		
Chest Chest movement, blunt trauma, open wounds, TIC		
Breath sounds present & equal?		
Percusses (PRN)		
Note heart sounds		
Abdomen Blunt trauma, penetrating wounds, distention		
Feel for tenderness		
Pelvis Deformity, penetrating wounds, TIC		
Extremities		
Lower - deformity, penetrating wounds, TIC		
Upper - deformity, penetrating wounds, TIC		

IF ALTERED MENTAL STATUS => DO BRIEF NEURO		
Pupils		
Glasgow Coma Scale		
Signs of Cushings Reflex Unresponsive, hypertensive, bradycardia		
Check for medical identification devices		
SAMPLE History		
Vital Signs BP, HR, Resp		
Make critical situation decision		
Examine posterior during roll - DCAP-BTLS		

ACTION	✓	COMMENTS
DETAILED HISTORY & PHYSICAL		
Obtain History & VS - may direct others to do . . . consider monitors		
Neurological Exam **LOC** - A.V.P.U.		
Pupils = or not =, response to light		
Motor fingers & toes move?		
Sensation touch fingers & toes		
If altered LOC: consider causes, do blood sugar		
Glasgow Coma Scale		
Signs of Cushings Reflex - unresponsive, hypertension, bradycardia		
Check for medical identification devices		
Head - scalp & face, DCAP-BTLS		
Battle signs and raccoon eyes		
Fluid drainage from ears or nose		
Pupils		
Skin color, condition, temperature		
Airway - open & clear?		
Signs of burns		
Breathing rate & quality		
Circulation - HR and quality		
Blood pressure		
Skin color, condition, temperature (if not done above)		
Neck - DCAP - BTLS		
Trachea		
Neck veins		
Chest - DCAPP - BTLS		
Breath sounds present & clear?		
Percusses (PRN)		
Heart sounds		
ET tube		
Abdomen - DCAP - BTLS		
Feel for tenderness		
Lower extremities DCAP-BTLS, PMS, ROM		
Upper extremities DCAP-BTLS, PMS, ROM		

GRADE KEY:

[✓] **Done, skill performed in sequence**
[D] **Delayed, performed too late or out of sequence**
[X] **Skill not performed or incorrectly**

5

Instructor Training Course

Affiliate faculty must teach the instructor course. This is generally a one-day course and may be taught the day before a scheduled provider course so that the instructor candidates can teach in the course and be monitored at that time.

MANDATORY TOPICS FOR A BTLS INSTRUCTOR COURSE

Introduction

Structure of BTLS program internationally and within the chapter
Chapter policy and procedures

Effective Teaching Techniques

How to teach
The bad lecture
The good lecture

Faculty Meetings

Precourse
Before skill stations
Before patient assessment teaching and testing
Postcourse

Moulage Techniques

Patient Assessment Stations

Instructor objectives
Setup
Techniques and troubleshooting
Grading criteria and grading sheets
Students must teach the skill stations

Mini-Lectures

Summary

The instructor candidates should receive continuing education credit for the number of hours of the course. Instructor candidates who attend a one-day instructor course will be monitored at future provider courses. If the instructor candidates attend an instructor course in conjunction with a provider course (three-day instructor course), they will be monitored during that course and receive certification at that time

SAMPLE AGENDA FOR ONE-DAY INSTRUCTOR COURSE

Registration — 30 min

Introduction to BTLS: — 30 min
  A. Structure of the BTLS
     program internationally
  B. Structure of the local BTLS chapter
  C. Chapter policies and procedures
  D. Obtaining authorization for a course
  E. Administrative guidelines
     1. Books
     2. Slides
     3. Precourse paperwork
     4. Course fees
     5. Postcourse paperwork

BTLS format — 30 min
  A. Faculty meetings
     1. Precourse
     2. Before skill stations
     3. Before patient assessment
        scenario teaching and testing
     4. Postcourse
  B. Lectures
  C. Skill stations
  D. Patient assessment scenario
     teaching and testing

Effective Teaching Techniques — 30 min
  A. How to teach
  B. The bad lecture
  C. The good lecture

Break — 15 min

Mini-lectures with review and feedback — 90 min

Lunch — 60 min

Moulage techniques — 60 min

Skill stations — 180 min (including 15-min break)
  A. Objectives
  B. Setting up
  C. Techniques and troubleshooting
  D. Grading criteria and grading sheets
  E. Students demonstrate teaching of skill stations

Wrap-up   15 min
Faculty meeting   30 min

INSTRUCTOR CANDIDATE MONITORING

At the first provider course after an instructor course, the instructor candidate should be paired with an experienced instructor during skill station teaching and patient assessment scenario teaching and testing. The chapter affiliate faculty member monitoring the course must have a list of the instructor candidates and observe them periodically during the course. At the conclusion of the postcourse faculty meeting, the chapter affiliate faculty member should meet separately with the instructors who were assigned instructor candidates to determine if the candidates should be certified or should be required to gain more experience. Feedback should be provided to the instructor candidates.

6

The Provider Course

SCENE SIZE-UP

BTLS instructors are responsible for knowing all the BTLS material to present their assigned topic in a simple and easily understood manner that ties in with the other parts of the BTLS method. The lectures are designed to present both basic and advanced information geared to the prehospital care of the trauma patient. Please keep this in mind as you give your lecture and refrain from adding unnecessary advanced material more applicable to the hospital environment. This may be modified if you are teaching hospital personnel. Feel free to add material that is practical and pertinent, but remember to keep the lecture within the time allotted. The students should have read and studied the chapters. When you lecture you should present, reinforce, and explain only the key concepts. The slide set no longer has separate slides for the basic BTLS course. If you are teaching EMT-Bs or first responders, please explain that the advanced procedures mentioned on the slides do not apply to them and they are not responsible for the material.

Chapter Objectives

Upon completion of this lecture, the student should be able to

1. Explain the relationship of time to patient survival and explain how this affects his actions at the scene.
2. Discuss the steps of the scene size-up.
3. List two basic mechanisms of motion injury.
4. Discuss mechanisms and settings for blunt versus penetrating trauma.
5. Identify the three collisions associated with a motor vehicle crash (MVC) and relate potential patient injuries to deformity of the vehicle, interior structures, and body structures.
6. Name five common forms of MVCs.
7. Describe the potential injuries associated with proper and improper use of seat restraints, head rests, and air bags in a head-on collision.
8. Differentiate lateral-impact collision from head-on collision based on the three collisions associated with an MVC.
9. Describe potential injuries from rear-end collisions.

10. Explain why the mortality rate is higher for victims ejected from vehicles in MVCs.

11. Describe the three assessment criteria for falls and relate them to anticipated injuries.

12. Identify the two most common forms of penetrating injuries and discuss associated mechanisms and extent of injury.

13. Relate three factors involved in blast injuries to patient assessment.

Key Lecture Points

1. Explain the relationship of time to patient survival and how this affects our actions at the scene.

2. Explain the steps of the scene size-up and the importance of each step.

3. Explain the importance of being aware of mechanisms of injury.

4. Briefly review the concept of transfer of energy.

5. Stress the concept of the "three collisions."

6. Briefly review the highlights of specific situations.
   Large Vehicle Accidents
       Frontal deceleration—effect on driver and passengers
       Lateral impact
       Rear impact
       Rollover
       Effect of restraints—lap belts, cross-chest-lap belts, and air bags
       Tractor accidents
   Small Vehicle Accidents
       Motorcycle
       All-terrain vehicles
       Personal watercraft
       Snowmobiles
   Pedestrian injuries
   Falls
   Penetrating injuries
   Knives
   Gunshot wounds
   Blast injury

ASSESSMENT AND INITIAL MANAGEMENT OF THE TRAUMA PATIENT

BTLS instructors are responsible for knowing all the BTLS material to present their assigned topic in a simple and easily understood manner that ties in with the other parts of the BTLS method. The lectures are designed to present both basic and advanced information geared to the prehospital care of the trauma patient. Please keep this in mind as you give your lecture and refrain from adding unnecessary advanced material more applicable to the hospital environment. This may be modified if you are teaching hospital EMS personnel. Feel free to add material that is practical and pertinent, but remember to keep the lecture within the time allotted. The students should have read and studied the chapters. When you lecture you should present, reinforce, and explain only the key concepts. The slide set no longer has separate slides for the basic BTLS course. If you are teaching EMT-Bs or first responders, please explain that the advanced procedures mentioned on the slides do not apply to them and they are not responsible for the material.

Chapter Objectives

Upon completion of this chapter, you should be able to

1. Describe the steps in trauma assessment and management.
2. Describe the initial assessment and explain how it relates to the BTLS rapid trauma survey and the focused exam.
3. Describe when the initial assessment can be interrupted.
4. Describe when critical interventions should be made and where to make them.
5. Identify which patients have critical conditions and how they should be managed.
6. Describe the detailed exam.
7. Describe the ongoing exam

Key Lecture Points

1. The concept of simultaneous assessment and intervention in life-threatening emergencies needs to be stressed; though it must be pointed out that the initial assessment is interrupted only for airway obstruction or the need to perform CPR.
2. The step-by-step assessment scheme must be taught.
3. Emphasize the need to get the critically injured patient out of the field and to an appropriate hospital as quickly as possible. The ten-minute rule must be reinforced.
4. Assessment priorities need to be established according to the ABC method.
5. Stress that the ongoing exam should be performed if the patient's condition deteriorates.

INITIAL AIRWAY MANAGEMENT

BTLS instructors are responsible for knowing all the BTLS material present their assigned topic in a simple and easily understood manner that ties in with the other parts of the BTLS method. The lectures are designed to present both basic and advanced information geared to the prehospital care of the trauma patient. Please keep this in mind as you give your lecture and refrain from adding unnecessary advanced material more applicable to the hospital environment. This may be modified if you are teaching hospital EMS personnel. Feel free to add material that is practical and pertinent, but remember to keep the lecture within the time allotted. The students should have read and studied the chapters. When you lecture you should present, reinforce, and explain only the key concepts. The slide set no longer has separate slides for the basic BTLS course. If you are teaching EMT-Bs or first responders, please explain that the advanced procedures mentioned on the slides do not apply to them and they are not responsible for the material.

Chapter Objectives

Upon completion of this lecture, the student should be able to

1. Describe the anatomy and physiology of the respiratory system.
2. Define the following terms:
   a. Hyperventilation
   b. Hypoventilation
   c. Tidal volume
   d. Minute volume
   e. Delivered volume
   f. Compliance
3. Explain the importance of observation as it relates to airway control.
4. Describe methods to deliver supplemental oxygen to the trauma patient.
5. Briefly describe the indications and contraindications and the advantages and disadvantages of the following airway adjuncts:
   a. Nasopharyngeal airways
   b. Oropharyngeal airways
   c. Bag-valve masks
   d. Oxygen-powered, flow-restricted ventilation devices
   e. Endotracheal intubation
6. Describe the Sellick maneuver.
7. Describe the essential contents of an airway kit.
8. Describe the pitfalls associated with airway management.

Key Lecture Points

1. The differences in airway management of the trauma patient as opposed to the medical patient need to be clearly emphasized. Particular emphasis needs to be placed on stabilizing the cervical spine and maintaining stability of the cervical spine during airway maneuvers.
2. C-spine control must be emphasized in any patient who is unconscious or who has an altered level of consciousness due either to head injury, drugs, or alcohol. It must be clearly understood and clearly stated that these patients may have altered perceptions of pain and therefore be un-

aware of their injury, be unable to splint the injury themselves, and be unable to direct attention to it.

3. It must be stressed that any movement, especially hyperextension of the cervical spine during airway maneuvers, may do great damage.

4. Continuous monitoring of the airway to provide necessary suction must be done.

5. High-flow oxygen (as close to 100 percent as possible) must be provided to trauma patients. Discuss oxygen settings.

6. Remind students that the oropharyngeal airway is for use only in the unconscious patient with no gag reflex.

7. Stress that oxygen-powered breathing devices are generally not used in trauma patients because their high pressure can cause lung injury. The new oxygen-powered, flow-restricted ventilation devices that are set to deliver a set flow of 40 L/min at a maximum pressure of 50+5 cm water are an exception. Recent studies suggest they are safe to use.

8. Review airway management in the conscious versus unconscious patient.

9. Review management of the prone patient and the patient with profuse upper airway bleeding.

THORACIC TRAUMA

BTLS instructors are responsible for knowing all the BTLS material to present their assigned topic in a simple and easily understood manner that ties in with the other parts of the BTLS method. The lectures are designed to present both basic and advanced information geared to the prehospital care of the trauma patient. Please keep this in mind as you give your lecture and refrain from adding unnecessary advanced material more applicable to the hospital environment. This may be modified if you are teaching hospital EMS personnel. Feel free to add material that is practical and pertinent, but remember to keep the lecture within the time allotted. The students should have read and studied the chapters. When you lecture you should present, reinforce, and explain only the key concepts. The slide set no longer has separate slides for the basic BTLS course. If you are teaching EMT-Bs or first responders, please explain that the advanced procedures mentioned on the slides do not apply to them and they are not responsible for the material.

Chapter Objectives

Upon completion of this lecture, the student should be able to

1. Identify the major symptoms of thoracic trauma.
2. Describe the signs of thoracic trauma.
3. State the immediate life-threatening thoracic injuries.
4. Explain the pathophysiology and management of an open pneumothorax.
5. Describe the clinical signs of a tension pneumothorax in conjunction with appropriate management.
6. List three indications to perform emergency chest decompression.
7. Explain the hypovolemic and respiratory compromise pathophysiology and management in massive hemothorax.
8. Define flail chest in relation to associated physical findings and management.
9. Identify the triad of physical findings in the diagnosis of cardiac tamponade.
10. Explain the cardiac involvement and management associated with blunt injury to the chest.
11. Summarize other injuries and their appropriate management.

Key Lecture Points

1. Briefly review the anatomy of the chest, particularly the great vessels.
2. Emphasize load-and-go conditions and discuss why these conditions are so critical:
   a. Massive hemothorax with shock: Explain that when massive hemothorax has occurred, as evidenced by dullness to percussion and diminished breath sounds in the base of the affected lung, massive hemorrhage has occurred into the chest with major blood vessel disruption and massive blood loss. If these patients are not rapidly taken to surgery, they usually die.
   b. Tension pneumothorax: Explain how the increased pressure in the chest reduces blood return to the heart, causing reduction in cardiac output, and thus producing shock. Stress the signs and symptoms of the tension pneumothorax (review the primary survey) and how critical it is not to leave out steps in the primary survey, which would prevent the identification of this problem.

c. Penetrating chest trauma with shock: Explain that the penetrating chest injury with resulting evidence of shock is a load-and-go situation because of the many serious and potentially lethal conditions that may result.

3. Discuss the mechanics of airflow during inspiration and expiration. Discuss how the presence of an open wound into the pleural space decreases air movement through the tracheobronchial tree.

4. Discuss the pathophysiology of the flail chest and the management of this problem: Assisted ventilation and prevention of movement of the flail segment if it is decreasing air movement through the tracheobronchial tree. Stress that hand stabilization is usually adequate until the patient is moved into the ambulance. Point out that nasotracheal intubation (patient usually has a gag reflex) is the most effective method to stabilize the flail and oxygenate the patient.

5. A review of the mechanism of injury in chest trauma is appropriate. Stress the importance of anticipating serious chest trauma or the potential for life-threatening injury even before deterioration has occurred. This is particularly important in those patients with evidence of major chest trauma.

SHOCK EVALUATION AND MANAGEMENT

BTLS instructors are responsible for knowing all the BTLS material to present their assigned topic in a simple and easily understood manner that ties in with the other parts of the BTLS method. The lectures are designed to present both basic and advanced information geared to the prehospital care of the trauma patient. Please keep this in mind as you give your lecture and refrain from adding unnecessary advanced material more applicable to the hospital environment. This may be modified if you are teaching hospital EMS personnel. Feel free to add material that is practical and pertinent, but remember to keep the lecture within the time allotted. The students should have already read and studied the chapters. When you lecture you should present, reinforce, and explain only the key concepts. The slide set no longer has separate slides for the basic BTLS course. If you are teaching EMT-Bs or first responders, please explain that the advanced procedures mentioned on the slides do not apply to them and they are not responsible for the material.

Chapter Objectives

Upon completion of this lecture, the student should be able to

1. List the four components necessary for normal tissue perfusion.
2. Describe symptoms and signs of hemorrhagic shock.
3. Explain the pathophysiology of hemorrhagic shock and compare to the pathophysiology of high-space shock.
4. Describe the three common clinical shock syndromes.
5. Describe the management of the following:
   a. Hemorrhage that can be controlled
   b. Hemorrhage that cannot be controlled
   c. Nonhemorrhagic shock syndromes
6. Discuss the routine priorities in the prehospital management of shock.
7. Discuss the current indications for the use of IV fluids in the treatment of hemorrhagic shock.
8. Discuss the current indications and contraindications for the use of the antishock garment in the treatment of traumatic shock.

Key Lecture Points

1. Discuss the modern concept of "shock": threat to normal cell function caused by diminished tissue perfusion and/or hypoxia.
2. Discuss the pathophysiology of hemorrhagic shock including the classic signs and symptoms and their cause.
3. Discuss the three shock syndromes:
   a. Low volume (absolute hypovolemia)
   b. High space (relative hypovolemia)
   c. Mechanical (obstructive)
4. Discuss the management of shock:
   a. Posttraumatic hemorrhage
      1. Exsanguinating external hemorrhage that can be controlled
      2. Exsanguinating external hemorrhage that cannot be controlled

3. Exsanguinating internal hemorrhage
   b. Nonhemorrhagic shock
      1. Mechanical shock
      2. High-space shock

5. Discuss the current status of the antishock garment.

6. Stress that shock is, in general, recognized too late and treated insufficiently. Point out that delaying transport of a patient in shock is a critical mistake.

HEAD TRAUMA

BTLS instructors are responsible for knowing all the BTLS material present their assigned topic in a simple and easily understood manner that ties in with the other parts of the BTLS method. The lectures are designed to present both basic and advanced information geared to the prehospital care of the trauma patient. Please keep this in mind as you give your lecture and refrain from adding unnecessary advanced material more applicable to the hospital environment. This may be modified if you are teaching hospital EMS personnel. Feel free to add material that is practical and pertinent, but remember to keep the lecture within the time allotted. The students should have read and studied the chapters. When you lecture you should present, reinforce, and explain only the key concepts. The slide set no longer has separate slides for the basic BTLS course. If you are teaching EMT-Bs or first responders, please explain that the advanced procedures mentioned on the slides do not apply to them and they are not responsible for the material.

Chapter Objectives

Upon completion of this lecture, the student should be able to

1. Describe the anatomy of the head and brain.
2. Describe the pathophysiology of traumatic brain injury.
3. Explain the difference between primary and secondary brain injury.
4. Describe the mechanisms for the development of secondary brain injury.
5. Describe the assessment of the patient with a head injury.
6. Describe the management of the patient with a head injury.
7. Describe the management of the cerebral herniation syndrome.
8. Identify potential problems in the management of the patient with a head injury.

Key Lecture Points

1. Cover the anatomy.
2. Cover the physiology of the brain and explain why hyperventilation is no longer recommended except in cases of herniation syndrome.
3. Emphasize the control of the airway in the patient with an altered level of consciousness. Stress that suction must be available at all times.
4. Stress that a patient with a serious head injury (Glasgow Coma Score of 8 or less) will not tolerate hypoxia or hypotension. In this situation do not allow the blood pressure to get below 100–110 systolic.
5. Mention that in the setting of shock in a patient with a head injury, the antishock garment is not contraindicated.
6. Mention the aspects of the Glasgow Coma Score. This score should always be recorded if there is altered mental status.
7. Stress indications for hyperventilation.

SPINAL TRAUMA

BTLS instructors are responsible for knowing all the BTLS material to present their assigned topic in a simple and easily understood manner that ties in with the other parts of the BTLS method. The lectures are designed to present both basic and advanced information geared to the prehospital care of the trauma patient. Please keep this in mind as you give your lecture and refrain from adding unnecessary advanced material more applicable to the hospital environment. This may be modified if you are teaching hospital EMS personnel. Feel free to add material that is practical and pertinent, but remember to keep the lecture within the time allotted. The students should have read and studied the chapters. When you lecture you should present, reinforce, and explain only the key concepts. The slide set no longer has separate slides for the basic BTLS course. If you are teaching EMT-Bs or first responders, please explain that the advanced procedures mentioned on the slides do not apply to them and they are not responsible for the material.

Chapter Objectives

Upon completion of this lecture, the student should be able to

1. Explain the normal anatomy and physiology of the spinal column and spinal cord.
2. Define *spinal motion restriction* (SMR) and explain why this term is preferred to the term *spinal immobilization.*
3. Describe the process of spinal immobilization from extrication through transportation, including airway maintenance.
4. Describe history and assessment criteria that identify patients who do not need spinal immobilization.
5. Give examples of special situations for which spinal immobilization techniques may need to be altered.
6. Using the clinical evaluation, differentiate neurogenic shock from hemorrhagic shock.

Key Lecture Points

1. Reinforce that any patient who has an altered level of consciousness must be presumed to have a cervical spine injury until proven otherwise. Appropriate precautions must be taken.
2. Stress that not only must the cervical spine be protected, but the entire spine, including the lumbar and dorsal spine.
3. Cover the anatomy of the spine briefly.
4. Briefly discuss the signs, symptoms, and treatment of neurogenic shock.
5. Begin use of the concept spinal motion restriction (SMR).
6. Stress documentation of the brief neurological exam (movement and sensation of hands and feet) before and after extrication or movement of the patient with a suspected spinal injury.
7. Stress that full SMR includes cervical collar, head immobilizer, and appropriate strapping applied to the patient on a long spine board.
8. Stress that cervical collars alone offer little to no protection of the C-spine. BTLS teaches that SMR is manually maintained by a team member until the patient is secured to the long spine board.

9. Emphasize that SMR on a long spineboard MANDATES airway protection by the rescuer due to the patient being prevented from protecting himself.

10. Note the indications for rapid extrication (without using short boards or KED-type devices). Primary survey of the patient identifies a condition that requires immediate intervention that cannot be done in the entrapped area, such as
   a. Airway obstruction that cannot be relieved by jaw thrust or finger sweep
   b. Cardiac or respiratory arrest
   c. Chest or airway injuries requiring ventilation or assisted ventilation
   d. Deep shock or bleeding that cannot be controlled

11. Note that there are other situations that are so desperate that you may not have time to use any technique and emergency rescue is warranted to pull the patient to safety. The need for emergency rescue is identified during the scene survey with circumstances that may immediately endanger the patient and the rescuers.
   a. Fire or immediate danger of fire
   b. Danger of explosion
   c. Rapidly rising water
   d. Structure in danger of collapse
   e. Continuing toxic exposure

12. Mention that KED-type devices may be difficult to apply and ineffective in pregnant and very obese patients.

13. Briefly clarify management of unusual circumstances, such as
   a. Closed space rescue
   b. Water rescue
   c. Prone and standing patients
   d. Pediatrics
   e. Geriatrics
   f. Helmet removal
   g. Obese patients
   h. Neck or face wounds

ABDOMINAL TRAUMA

BTLS instructors are responsible for knowing all the BTLS material to present their assigned topic in a simple and easily understood manner that ties in with the other parts of the BTLS method. The lectures are designed to present both basic and advanced information geared to the prehospital care of the trauma patient. Please keep this in mind as you give your lecture and refrain from adding unnecessary advanced material more applicable to the hospital environment. This may be modified if you are teaching hospital EMS personnel. Feel free to add material that is practical and pertinent, but remember to keep the lecture within the time allotted. The students should have read and studied the chapters. When you lecture you should present, reinforce, and explain only the key concepts. The slide set no longer has separate slides for the basic BTLS course. If you are teaching EMT-Bs or first responders, please explain that the advanced procedures mentioned on the slides do not apply to them and they are not responsible for the material.

Chapter Objectives

Upon completion of this lecture, the student should be able to

1. Identify the basic anatomy of the abdomen and explain how abdominal and chest injuries may be related.
2. Relate how injuries apparent on the exterior of the abdomen can damage underlying structures.
3. Differentiate between blunt and penetrating injuries and identify complications associated with each.
4. Describe possible intraperitoneal injuries based on findings of history, physical examination, and mechanism of injury.
5. Describe the treatment required for the patient with protruding viscera.
6. Discuss advanced life support interventions for patients with abdominal injuries.

Key Lecture Points

1. Cover the anatomy of the abdomen.
2. Stress the importance of the abdomen as regards morbidity and mortality associated with major trauma.
3. Mention that a distended abdomen is a very late sign in exsanguination within the abdomen.
4. Mention that abdominal trauma with shock is a grim finding and must be rapidly managed.
5. Discuss pelvic fractures and their potential for massive bleeding.
6. Mention that the antishock garment has not been shown to increase survival when used for shock from abdominal trauma and may actually increase internal bleeding.

EXTREMITY TRAUMA

BTLS instructors are responsible for knowing all the BTLS material to present their assigned topic in a simple and easily understood manner that ties in with the other parts of the BTLS method. The lectures are designed to present both basic and advanced information geared to the prehospital care of the trauma patient. Please keep this in mind as you give your lecture and refrain from adding unnecessary advanced material more applicable to the hospital environment. This may be modified if you are teaching hospital EMS personnel. Feel free to add material that is practical and pertinent, but remember to keep the lecture within the time allotted. The students should have read and studied the chapters. When you lecture you should present, reinforce, and explain only the key concepts. The slide set no longer has separate slides for the basic BTLS course. If you are teaching EMT-Bs or first responders, please explain that the advanced procedures mentioned on the slides do not apply to them and they are not responsible for the material.

Chapter Objectives

Upon completion of this lecture, the student should be able to

1. Prioritize extremity trauma in the assessment and management of life-threatening injuries.
2. Discuss the major complications and treatment of the following extremity injuries:
   a. Fractures
   b. Dislocations
   c. Amputations
   d. Open wounds
   e. Neurovascular injuries
   f. Sprains and strains
   g. Impaled objects
   h. Compartment syndrome
3. Estimate blood loss from pelvic and extremity fractures.
4. Discuss major mechanisms of injury, associated trauma, potential complications, and management of injury to the following areas:
   a. Pelvis
   b. Femur
   c. Hip
   d. Knee
   e. Tibia/fibula
   f. Clavicle and shoulder
   g. Forearm and wrist
   h. Hand or foot

Key Lecture Points

1. Stress that the extremities MUST be examined for exsanguinating blood loss during the BTLS primary survey.
2. The treatment of extremity trauma should be deemphasized in the patient with a load-and-go condition. In this scenario, traction splints should not be applied; but rather, a long spine board should be employed.

3. Estimated blood loss in major extremity fractures should be covered.

4. The splints available for various purposes should be mentioned.

5. Stress that the rescuer must note neurovascular status of the extremities before and after splinting procedures.

BURNS

BTLS instructors are responsible for knowing all the BTLS material to present their assigned topic in a simple and easily understood manner that ties in with the other parts of the BTLS method. The lectures are designed to present both basic and advanced information geared to the prehospital care of the trauma patient. Please keep this in mind as you give your lecture and refrain from adding unnecessary advanced material more applicable to the hospital environment. This may be modified if you are teaching hospital EMS personnel. Feel free to add material that is practical and pertinent, but remember to keep the lecture within the time allotted. The students should have read and studied the chapters. When you lecture you should present, reinforce, and explain only the key concepts. The slide set no longer has separate slides for the basic BTLS course. If you are teaching EMT-Bs or first responders, please explain that the advanced procedures mentioned on the slides do not apply to them and they are not responsible for the material.

Chapter Objectives

Upon completion of this lecture, the student should be able to

1. Identify the basic anatomy of the skin, including
   a. Epidermal and dermal layers
   b. Structures found within the skin
2. List the basic functions of the skin.
3. Identify the descriptive categories of burns.
4. Identify complications and describe the management of
   a. Thermal burns
   b. Chemical burns
   c. Electrical burns
   d. Lightning burns
   e. Pediatric burns
5. List situations and physical signs that may indicate
   a. Upper airway injury
   b. Inhalation injury
6. List signs and symptoms of carbon monoxide poisoning.
7. Discuss how carbon monoxide causes hypoxia.
8. Describe the treatment of carbon monoxide poisoning.
9. Estimate the depth of a burn based on skin appearance.
10. Estimate extent of a burn using the rule of nines.
11. Identify which patients may require transport to a burn center.

Key Lecture Points

1. Review the types and classifications of burns.
2. Discuss the management of different types of burns. Note should be made that while the burns should be cooled briefly to control ongoing heat injury, burns should not be subjected to prolonged cold exposure due to the risk of hypothermia.
3. Discuss the complications of major burns, such as airway compromise and later fluid loss.

4. Discuss the need to consider the mechanism of injury, especially with regard to the potential for carbon monoxide or other toxic gas inhalation. A note should be made as to whether this injury occurred in an enclosed space.

5. Stress the need for maintaining body temperature.

6. Discuss the treatment of carbon monoxide poisoning. Unless otherwise indicated, 100 percent oxygen should be used in the major burn patient until he can be further evaluated.

7. Discuss the findings that suggest inhalation injury and stress that the rescuer must always be alert to this injury.

8. Stress that the rescuer must record the time that the burn occurred.

9. Review chemical burns and how their treatment differs from thermal burns.

10. Review electrical burns and lightning burns and discuss their treatment.

11. Stress the danger of becoming a victim when dealing with electrical burns.

12. Mention that the rescuers should be alert to the signs of child abuse when dealing with burned children.

TRAUMA IN CHILDREN

BTLS instructors are responsible for knowing all the BTLS material to present their assigned topic in a simple and easily understood manner that ties in with the other parts of the BTLS method. The lectures are designed to present both basic and advanced information geared to the prehospital care of the trauma patient. Please keep this in mind as you give your lecture and refrain from adding unnecessary advanced material more applicable to the hospital environment. This may be modified if you are teaching hospital EMS personnel. Feel free to add material that is practical and pertinent, but remember to keep the lecture within the time allotted. The students should have read and studied the chapters. When you lecture you should present, reinforce, and explain only the key concepts. The slide set no longer has separate slides for the basic BTLS course. If you are teaching EMT-Bs or first responders, please explain that the advanced procedures mentioned on the slides do not apply to them and they are not responsible for the material.

Chapter Objectives

Upon completion of this lecture, the student should be able to

1. Describe effective techniques for gaining the confidence of children and their parents.
2. Predict pediatric injuries based on common mechanisms of injury.
3. Describe the primary survey and detailed exam in the pediatric patient.
4. Demonstrate understanding of the need for immediate transport in potentially life-threatening circumstances, regardless of lack of immediate parental consent.
5. Differentiate equipment needs of pediatric patients from those of adults.
6. Describe the various ways to immobilize a child and how this differs from an adult.
7. Discuss the need for involvement of EMS personnel in prevention programs for parents and children.

Key Lecture Points

1. Discuss the differences and similarities between the adult and pediatric patient as regards trauma management.
2. Cover the various baseline vital signs expected for the different age groups.
3. Note that the BTLS primary survey sequence is the same for pediatric as for adult patients.
4. Note that children will appear to be stable with fewer warning signs of deterioration, which can be followed by sudden disastrous decompensation.
5. Mention that gastric distension in small children may cause hypotension.
6. It may be mentioned that transport of small children in their car seats with appropriate additional stabilization may be acceptable.

TRAUMA IN THE ELDERLY

BTLS instructors are responsible for knowing all the BTLS material to present their assigned topic in a simple and easily understood manner that ties in with the other parts of the BTLS method. The lectures are designed to present both basic and advanced information geared to the prehospital care of the trauma patient. Please keep this in mind as you give your lecture and refrain from adding unnecessary advanced material more applicable to the hospital environment. This may be modified if you are teaching hospital EMS personnel. Feel free to add material that is practical and pertinent, but remember to keep the lecture within the time allotted. The students should have read and studied the chapters. When you lecture you should present, reinforce, and explain only the key concepts. The slide set no longer has separate slides for the basic BTLS course. If you are teaching EMT-Bs or first responders, please explain that the advanced procedures mentioned on the slides do not apply to them and they are not responsible for the material.

Chapter Objectives

Upon completion of this lecture, the student should be able to

1. Describe the changes that occur with aging, and explain how these changes can affect your assessment of the geriatric trauma patient.
2. Describe the assessment of the geriatric trauma patient.
3. Describe the treatment of the geriatric trauma patient.

Key Lecture Points

1. Review pathophysiology of aging by systems.
2. Stress that when doing field triage, the geriatric patients have more injuries and worse outcomes than younger patients who are subjected to the same mechanisms.
3. Review patient assessment and relate how aging affects assessment and interventions.
4. Discuss potential problems with spinal motion restriction in elderly patients.

TRAUMA IN PREGNANCY

BTLS instructors are responsible for knowing all the BTLS material to present their assigned topic in a simple and easily understood manner that ties in with the other parts of the BTLS method. The lectures are designed to present both basic and advanced information geared to the prehospital care of the trauma patient. Please keep this in mind as you give your lecture and refrain from adding unnecessary advanced material more applicable to the hospital environment. This may be modified if you are teaching hospital EMS personnel. Feel free to add material that is practical and pertinent, but remember to keep the lecture within the time allotted. The students should have read and studied the chapters. When you lecture you should present, reinforce, and explain only the key concepts. The slide set no longer has separate slides for thebasic BTLS course. If you are teaching EMT-Bs or first responders, please explain that the advanced procedures mentioned on the slides do not apply to them and they are not responsible for the material.

Chapter Objectives

Upon completion of this lecture, the student should be able to

1. Understand the dual goals in managing the pregnant trauma patient.
2. Describe the physiological changes associated with pregnancy.
3. Understand the pregnant trauma patient's response to hypovolemia.
4. Describe the types of injuries most commonly associated with the pregnant trauma patient.
5. Describe the initial assessment and management of the pregnant trauma patient.
6. Discuss trauma prevention in pregnancy.

Key Lecture Points

1. Cover the general information included in the lecture slides, including the information associated with the various trimesters.
2. Note should be made that the status of the fetus generally depends on the well-being of the mother. Therefore, if the mother has adequate blood volume, blood pressure, and circulation, then the fetus will do well. Use the quote "Death of the fetus in the trauma situation is most often associated with the death of the mother."
3. Mention that the treatment of shock is the same for pregnant patients as for other patients.
4. Emphasize that the physiologic changes of pregnancy may cause delay in the diagnosis of the shock state in the mother.
5. Stress that uterine obstruction of venous blood flow may cause hypotension in the supine patient ("supine hypotension syndrome") and thus must be prevented by rolling the patient or backboard to the left.
6. Mention that acute traumatic placental separation is fairly rare. The fetus is floating in a "shock absorber" of amniotic fluid, and the amount of blunt force necessary to injure the fetus is larger than might be expected.
7. Note that there is an increased rate of fetal demise two or three days following major trauma to the mother.
8. Mention that the KED may be ineffective as a short spinal immobilization device in the pregnant patient because of the difficulty with adequately securing the straps. This concern also applies to the very obese patient.

PATIENTS UNDER THE INFLUENCE OF ALCOHOL OR DRUGS

BTLS instructors are responsible for knowing all the BTLS material to present their assigned topic in a simple and easily understood manner that ties in with the other parts of the BTLS method. The lectures are designed to present both basic and advanced information geared to the prehospital care of the trauma patient. Please keep this in mind as you give your lecture and refrain from adding unnecessary advanced material more applicable to the hospital environment. This may be modified if you are teaching hospital EMS personnel. Feel free to add material that is practical and pertinent, but remember to keep the lecture within the time allotted. The students should have read and studied the chapters. When you lecture you should present, reinforce, and explain only the key concepts. The slide set no longer has separate slides for the basic BTLS course. If you are teaching EMT-Bs or first responders, please explain that the advanced procedures mentioned on the slides do not apply to them and they are not responsible for the material.

Chapter Objectives

Upon completion of this lecture, the student should be able to

1. List signs and symptoms of patients under the influence of alcohol and/or drugs.
2. Describe the five strategies you would use to best ensure cooperation during assessment and management of a patient under the influence of alcohol and/or drugs.
3. Describe situations in which you would restrain patients and tell how to handle an uncooperative patient.
4. List the special considerations for assessment and management of patients in whom substance abuse is suspected.

Key Lecture Points

1. Review commonly abused drugs and their common signs and symptoms.
2. Review clues of drug use by the patient.
3. Review the pertinent history you should obtain when managing a patient who may be under the influence of drugs.
4. Explain how to interact with a patient who is under the influence of drugs.
5. Explain how to manage the patient who is injured, under the influence and uncooperative. Be familiar with local laws regarding restraining a patient.

THE TRAUMA CARDIOPULMONARY ARREST

BTLS instructors are responsible for knowing all the BTLS material to present their assigned topic in a simple and easily understood manner that ties in with the other parts of the BTLS method. The lectures are designed to present both basic and advanced information geared to the prehospital care of the trauma patient. Please keep this in mind as you give your lecture and refrain from adding unnecessary advanced material more applicable to the hospital environment. This may be modified if you are teaching hospital EMS personnel. Feel free to add material that is practical and pertinent, but remember to keep the lecture within the time allotted. The students should have read and studied the chapters. When you lecture you should present, reinforce, and explain only the key concepts. The slide set no longer has separate slides for the basic BTLS course. If you are teaching EMT-Bs or first responders, please explain that the advanced procedures mentioned on the slides do not apply to them and they are not responsible for the material.

Chapter Objectives

Upon completion of this lecture, the student should be able to

1. Identify treatable causes of traumatic cardiopulmonary arrest.
2. Describe the proper evaluation and management of the patient in traumatic cardiopulmonary arrest.

Key Lecture Points

1. Briefly review the causes of cardiopulmonary arrest in the trauma situation.
2. Review the general management of the trauma arrest.
3. Compare and contrast the management of the trauma arrest to general advanced cardiac resuscitation guidelines.
4. Remind the students always to think of hemorrhagic shock, tension pneumothorax, and pericardial tamponade when evaluating the trauma arrest patient.
5. Stress rapid transport of the trauma arrest patient.

BLOOD AND BODY SUBSTANCE PRECAUTIONS IN THE PREHOSPITAL SETTING

BTLS instructors are responsible for knowing all the BTLS material to present their assigned topic in a simple and easily understood manner that ties in with the other parts of the BTLS method. The lectures are designed to present both basic and advanced information geared to the prehospital care of the trauma patient. Please keep this in mind as you give your lecture and refrain from adding unnecessary advanced material more applicable to the hospital environment. This may be modified if you are teaching hospital EMS personnel. Feel free to add material that is practical and pertinent, but remember to keep the lecture within the time allotted. The students should have read and studied the chapters. When you lecture you should present, reinforce, and explain only the key concepts. The slide set no longer has separate slides for the basic BTLS course. If you are teaching EMT-Bs or first responders, please explain that the advanced procedures mentioned on the slides do not apply to them and they are not responsible for the material.

Chapter Objectives

Upon completion of this lecture, the student should be able to

1. State the three most common blood-borne viral illnesses that EMS providers are most likely to be exposed to in the provision of patient care.
2. Discuss the signs and symptoms of tuberculosis and describe protective measures to take to reduce possible exposure to TB.
3. Describe precautions EMS providers can take to prevent exposure to blood and other potentially infectious materials (cerebrospinal fluid [CSF], synovial fluid, amniotic fluid, pericardial fluid, pleural fluid, or any fluid with gross visible blood).
4. Identify appropriate use of personal protective equipment.
5. Describe procedures for EMS providers to follow if they are accidentally exposed.

Key Lecture Points

1. Explain that trauma care involves exposure to blood and body fluids and to the diseases that are spread by these means.
2. Explain the difference between active and passive immunity.
3. Describe the diseases caused by Hepatitis B, Hepatitis C, and HIV.
4. Discuss tuberculosis and why it is making a comeback.
5. Explain precautions to prevent contracting these diseases.
6. Describe the procedures to follow if accidentally exposed to blood or body fluids.

SKILL STATION 1—BASIC AND ADVANCED AIRWAY MANAGEMENT

Before beginning, review pages 51–52 in your instructor guide. Minimum instructors needed: 2

Objectives

At the conclusion of this station, the student should be able to

1. Perform the various manual methods of opening the airway.
2. Suction the airway.
3. Insert a nasopharyngeal and oropharyngeal airway.
4. Ventilate using the pocket mask.
5. Ventilate using the bag-valve device.
6. Correctly use a pulse oximeter.
7. Describe the preparations necessary to perform endotracheal intubation.
8. Perform adult and infant orotracheal laryngoscopic intubation.
9. Perform nasotracheal intubation.
10. Confirm correct tube placement.
11. Anchor the endotracheal tube.

Skill 1A—Basic Airway Management

Important Points

1. Show the students how to set up and connect the reducing valve on an oxygen cylinder (review the procedure beforehand).
2. Demonstrate how much easier it is to give adequate ventilation using mouth-to-mask ventilation rather than bag-valve-mask ventilation.
3. Stress that using the reservoir bag with the bag-valve device will double the oxygen concentration to the patient.
4. Stress how to interpret the pulse oximeter reading and also those conditions that make pulse oximeter reading unreliable.
5. If you have time, you may demonstrate new or different equipment.

Equipment List

Item	Quantity
CPR mannequin	1 or 2
Portable suction machine with charger	1 or 2
Manual suction device (optional)	1 or 2
Suction tubing 1 or 2	
Tonsil suction tips (Yaunker)	1 or 2
Tongue blades	10

Silicone lubricant spray (cans)	1
Nasopharyngeal airways (various sizes)	1 set
Oropharyngeal airways (various sizes)	1 set
Pocket masks (with supplemental oxygen nipple)	2
Oxygen cylinders	2
Pulse oximeters	1 or 2
Oxygen connecting tubing	3
Reducing valves for cylinders	3
Stands for cylinders	3
Adult bag-valve device with adult face mask	2
Pediatric bag-valve device	1
Children's face masks (various sizes)	1 set
Reservoir bags for bag-valve devices	3
Adult intubation mannequin	1
Pediatric intubation mannequin	1
Assorted endotracheal tubes	3 or 4
Jar of water	1
Tables	2

Procedures

I. Manual techniques to open the airway
  A. Modified jaw thrust
    1. Place your hands on either side of the neck at the base of the skull.
    2. While maintaining in-line stabilization of the neck, push up on the angles of the mandible with your thumbs.
  B. Jaw thrust
    1. Stabilize the head and neck with your knees or have your partner stabilize the neck in a neutral position.
    2. Using the index and middle fingers of each hand, grasp the angles of the jaw just below the ear.
    3. Lift gently.
  C. Chin lift
    1. Stabilize the head and neck with your knees or have your partner stabilize the neck in a neutral position.
    2. Place the fingers on one hand under the chin.
    3. With the thumb of the same hand, grasp the chin below the lower lip.
    4. Lift gently.
  D. Jaw lift (used for inserting oral airway or BIAD)
    1. Stabilize the head and neck with your knees or have your partner stabilize the neck in a neutral position.
    2. Place the fingers of one hand under the chin.
    3. Insert the thumb of the same hand inside the mouth. Grasp the lower incisors.
    4. Lift gently.

II. Suctioning the airway
   A. Attach the suction tubing to the portable suction machine.
   B. Turn the device on and test it.
   C. Insert the suction tube through the nose or mouth without activating the suction.
   D. Activate the suction and withdraw the suction tube using circular movements.
   E. Repeat the procedure as necessary.

III. Insertion of pharyngeal airways
   A. Nasopharyngeal airway
      1. Choose the appropriate size. It should be the largest that will fit easily through the external nares.
      2. Lubricate the tube.
      3. Insert it straight back through the right nostril with the beveled edge of the airway toward the septum.
      4. To insert it in the left nostril, turn the airway upside down so that the bevel is toward the septum, then insert straight back through the nostril until you reach the posterior pharynx. At this point, turn the airway 180 degrees and insert it down the pharynx until it lies behind the tongue.
   B. Oropharyngeal airway
      1. Choose the appropriate size. Demonstrate how to measure from the lips to the ear lobe or angle of the jaw.
      2. Open the airway
         a. Scissor maneuver
         b. Jaw lift
         c. Tongue blade
      3. Insert the airway gently without pushing the tongue back into the pharynx.
         a. Insert the airway upside down and rotate into place. This method should not be used in children.
         b. Insert the airway under direct vision using the tongue blade.

IV. Use of pocket mask with supplemental oxygen
   A. Have your partner stabilize the neck in a neutral position (or apply a good stabilization device).
   B. Connect the oxygen tubing to the oxygen cylinder and the mask.
   C. Open the oxygen cylinder and set the flow rate at 12 liters/min.
   D. Open the airway.
   E. Insert the oral airway properly
   F. Place the mask on the face and establish a good seal.
   G. Ventilate mouth-to-mask with 800 to 1000 cc each breath.

V. Use of the bag-valve mask
   A. Stabilize the neck with a suitable device.
   B. Connect the oxygen tubing to the bag-valve system and oxygen cylinder.
   C. Attach the oxygen reservoir to the bag-valve mask.
   D. Open the oxygen cylinder and set the flow rate at 12 liters/mm.
   E. Select the proper size mask and attach it to the bag-valve device.
   F. Open the airway.
   G. Insert the oral airway properly.
   H. Place the mask on the face and have your partner establish and maintain a good seal.
   I. Using both hands, ventilate with about 800 cc of volume with each breath.

J. If you are forced to ventilate without a partner, use one hand to maintain a face seal and the other to squeeze the bag. This decreases the volume of ventilation because less volume is produced by only one hand squeezing the bag.

VI. Use of the bag-valve mask to ventilate infants (optional)
   A. Stabilize the neck with a suitable device.
   B. Connect the oxygen tubing to the bag-valve system and oxygen cylinder.
   C. Attach the oxygen reservoir to the bag-valve mask.
   D. Open the oxygen cylinder and set the flow rate at 12 liters/mm.
   E. Select the proper size mask and attach it to the bag-valve device.
   F. Open the airway.
   G. Insert the oral airway properly.
   H. Place the mask on the face and establish and maintain a good seal. You may have to turn the mask upside down to get a good seal.
   I. Ventilate with enough volume to make the chest rise. Use about 20 centimeters of water pressure. To experience this amount of pressure place a 20 cm (#8) endotracheal tube vertically in water except for the bag connection and compress the resuscitation bag so that air bubbles come out the tower end of the endotracheal tube. This will be 20 cm of water pressure. Pressures higher than this will always cause some air to be forced into the stomach.

VII. Use of the pulse oximeter

A pulse oximeter is a noninvasive photoelectric device that measures the arterial oxygen saturation and pulse rate in the peripheral circulation. It consists of a portable monitor and a sensing probe that clips onto the patient's finger, toe, or earlobe. The device displays the pulse rate and the arterial oxygen saturation in a percentage value ($\%SaO_2$). This is a very useful device that should be used on all patients with any type of respiratory compromise. The pulse oximeter is useful to assess the patient's respiratory status, the effectiveness of oxygen therapy, and the effectiveness of BVM or FROPVD ventilation. Remember that the device measures $\%SaO_2$, not the arterial partial pressure of oxygen (PaO_2).

The hemoglobin molecule is so efficient at carrying oxygen that it is 90 percent saturated ($90\%SaO_2$) when the partial pressure of oxygen is only 60 mm Hg (100 is normal). If you are used to thinking about PaO_2 (where 90–100 mm Hg is normal), then you may be fooled into thinking that a SaO_2 reading (pulse oximeter) of 90 percent is normal when it is actually critically low. As a general rule, any pulse oximeter reading below 92 percent is cause for concern and requires some sort of intervention (open airway, suction, oxygen, assisted ventilation, intubation, decompression of tension pneumothorax, etc.). A pulse oximeter reading below 90 percent is critical and requires *immediate* intervention to maintain adequate tissue oxygenation. Try to maintain a pulse oximeter reading above 95 percent or higher. However, do not withhold oxygen from a patient with a pulse oximeter reading above 95 percent who also shows signs and symptoms of hypoxia or difficulty breathing.

The following are conditions that make the pulse oximeter reading unreliable:

1. Poor peripheral perfusion (shock, vasoconstriction, hypotension). Do not attach the sensing probe onto an injured extremity. Try not to use the sensing probe on the same arm that you are using to monitor the blood pressure. Be aware that the pulse oximeter reading will go down while the blood pressure cuff is inflated.

2. Severe anemia.

3. Carbon monoxide poisoning. This will give falsely high readings since the sensing probe cannot distinguish between oxyhemoglobin and carboxyhemoglobin.

4. Hypothermia.

5. Excessive patient movement.

6. High ambient light (bright sunlight, high-intensity light on area of the sensing probe).

7. Nail polish or a dirty fingernail if you are using a finger probe. Use acetone to clean the nail before attaching the probe.

Procedure

Turn on the device.

A. Clean the area (earlobe, fingernail, and toenail) that you are to monitor.

B. Attach the sensing clip to the area.

C. Note the reading on the device.

Basic Skill 1B—Assisting with Advanced Airway Management

Note: This skill is taught only to students taking the basic BTLS course. It consists of

1. Preparation for endotracheal intubation (see skill 1C)

2. Procedure for assisting with orotracheal and nasotracheal intubation (see below)

3. Confirmation of tube placement (see skill 1E)

4. Anchoring the tube (see skill 1F)

Equipment

The same as for skill 1D

Procedure

1. Following ventilation and initial preparations, the student should hold the patient's head and/or perform the Sellick maneuver. The student should count slowly aloud to 30 as the ALS provider performs the intubation.

2. When the tube is inserted, the student (or the ALS provider) should check the tube for placement by the confirmation protocol (skill 1E).

3. When the tube placement is confirmed, the student should anchor the tube (skill 1F).

ADVANCED AIRWAY MANAGEMENT

Advanced Skill 1C—Preparation for Endotracheal Intubation

Whatever the method of intubation used, both patients and rescuers should be prepared for the procedure. The following are considered basic to all intubation procedures:

1. Gloves: Rubber examining (not necessarily sterile) gloves should be worn for all intubation procedures

2. Eye protection: Goggles or face shield should be worn to protect from blood or fluids that might be coughed up

3. Oxygenation: All patients should be ventilated, or should breathe high-flow oxygen (12 L/min) for several minutes prior to the attempt.

4. Airway equipment: All equipment should have been checked and should be kept at hand in an organized kit. For laryngoscopic intubation, the endotracheal tube should be held in a "field hockey stick" or open "J" shape by a malleable stylet that is first lubricated and inserted until the distal end is just proximal to the side-hole of the endotracheal tube. The cuff of the endotracheal tube should be checked by inflating it with 10 cc of air. The air should then be *completely* removed and the syringe filled with air left attached to the pilot tube. The cuff and distal end of the tube is then lubricated.

5. Suction: Must be immediately at hand.

6. Assistant: An assistant (may be an EMT-B or first responder) should be available to help in the procedure. The Sellick maneuver should be applied during ventilation and the subsequent intubation attempt. The assistant may also aid in holding the head and neck immobile and informing you when thirty seconds have elapsed.

Optional Preparation

7. Lidocaine: Intravenous lidocaine, given 4–5 minutes before intubation attempts, has been shown to decrease the adverse cardiovascular and intracranial pressure effects of the intubation procedure. *If time permits,* an IV bolus of 1–1.5 mg/kg may be given to all adult patients prior to intubation or suctioning.

Advanced Skill 1D—Laryngoscopic Orotracheal Intubation

Important Points

1. Check batteries and all laryngoscope lights.

2. Since this is a trauma course, cervical collars should be applied to the intubation mannequins so the students can learn to intubate without extending the neck. Have one student stabilize the neck from below while another intubates.

3. Require the students to follow the procedure as outlined in the text. The suction machine can be simulated but the tubing and suction tip should be placed next to the patient each time intubation is practiced.

Equipment List

Item	Quantity
Adult intubation mannequins	2
Infant intubation mannequins	2
Adult cuffed ET tubes	
7 mm	2
8 mm	2
9 mm	2
Pediatric ET tubes (not cuffed)	
3.5 mm	2

4.0 mm	2
4.5 mm	2
Wire guides for adult ET tubes	2
Wire guides for pediatric tubes	2
Laryngoscope handles	4
Spare batteries for laryngoscopes	8
Spare bulbs for laryngoscopes	4
Adult laryngoscope blades	
Curved	2
Straight	2
Pediatric laryngoscope blades	
Straight	2
Can of silicone lubricant spray	1
10-cc syringes	2
Lighted stylet (optional)	2
Oral airways (size to fit adult mannequin)	2
Oral airways (size to fit infant mannequin)	2
Tonsil auctions tip (Yaunker) and suction tubing	4 each
Bag-valve devices	4
Nonsterile rubber gloves	1 box
Face shields or goggles	4
CO_2 detector (optional)	1
Esophageal detection device (optional)	1

Procedure—Adult Endotracheal Intubation

In this method, the upper airway and the glottic opening are visualized and the tube is slipped gently through the cords. Its advantages include the ability to see obstructions and to visualize the accurate placement of the tube. It has the disadvantage of requiring a relatively relaxed (unconscious) patient without anatomic distortion and with minimal bleeding or secretions.

1. Stabilize the neck in a neutral position from below (done by your partner).
2. While the patient is being ventilated, prepare your equipment:
    a. Be sure suction apparatus is available and functioning.
    b. Select the correct size ET tube, insert a wire guide, attach a 10-cc syringe, and test the cuff.
    c. Connect the laryngoscope blade and handle. Test the light.

Following ventilation and initial preparations, the following steps should be carried out:

1. An assistant holds the head, performs the Sellick maneuver, and counts slowly aloud to 30 (if the intubator requests).

2. Holding the laryngoscope in the left hand, the intubator pulls down on the chin and slides the blade into the right side of the patient's mouth, pushing the tongue to the left and "inching" the blade down along the tongue in an attempt to see the epiglottis. A key maneuver must be performed here: the blade must pull forward on the tongue to lift up the epiglottis and bring it into view.

3. The laryngoscope blade is used to lift the tongue and epiglottis up and forward in a straight line. "Levering" the blade is a common error with novices and can result in broken teeth and other trauma. The laryngoscope is essentially a "hook" to lift the tongue and epiglottis up and out of the way so that the glottic opening can be identified.

4. The tube is advanced along the right side of the oropharynx once the epiglottis is seen. When the glottic opening (or even just the arytenoid cartilages) is identified, the tube is slipped through to a depth of about 5 cm beyond the cords.

5. While the tube is still held firmly, the cuff is inflated with 4 to 6 cc of air and ventilation begun.

6. Insert an oral airway.

7. The tube is then checked for placement by the confirmation protocol and secured in place.

8. Begin ventilation using adequate oxygen concentration and tidal volume.

Procedure—Infant Endotracheal Intubation

Follow the same procedure as for adults, except that there is no cuff to inflate.

Advanced Skill 1E—Confirmation of Tube Placement

Although the most reliable method of ensuring proper placement is actually visualizing the tube passing through the glottic opening, this is often a luxury we cannot always count on in the trauma patient. Visualization of the arytenoids is perhaps as much as we can expect, especially in a patient whose head and neck are immobilized and at risk if moved.

A simple yet effective protocol for tube confirmation is possible and practical. Such a protocol should recognize the unreliable nature of auscultation as the sole method of confirming intratracheal placement. Correct intratracheal placement should be suspected from the following initial signs:

1. An anteriorward displacement of the laryngeal prominence as the tube is passed distally.

2. Coughing, bucking, or straining on the part of the patient.

Note: Phonation (any noise made with the vocal cords) is ABSOLUTE EVIDENCE THAT THE TUBE IS IN THE ESOPHAGUS AND SHOULD BE REMOVED IMMEDIATELY.

3. Breath condensation on the tube with each ventilation. This is not 100 precent reliable but is very suggestive of intratracheal placement.

4. Normal compliance with bag ventilation—the bag does not suddenly "collapse," but rather there is some resilience to it and resistance to lung inflation.

5. No air leak around the cuff after inflation; persistent leak indicates esophageal intubation until proven otherwise.

The following procedure should then be **immediately** carried out to prove correct placement:

1. Auscultate three sites:
   a. The epigastrium (perhaps the most important site) should be silent, with no sounds heard.

b. Right and left midaxillary lines.

2. Inspect: Observe full movement of the chest with ventilation. Watch for any change in the patient's color or in the pulse oximeter reading. Also observe the EKG monitor for changes.

When you perform the detailed assessment, or when there is a question of correct tube placement after the above confirmation protocol, you should

1. Auscultate six sites:
   a. The epigastrium. It should be silent, with no sounds heard.
   b. Right and left apex.
   c. Right and left midaxillary lines.
   d. The sternal notch. "Tracheal" sounds should be readily heard here.

2. Inspect the chest for full movement of the chest with ventilation.

3. Gently palpate the tube cuff in the sternal notch while compressing the pilot balloon between the fingers and thumb; a pressure wave should be felt in the sternal notch.

4. Use adjuncts such as a CO_2 detector (capnographic or colormetric), esophageal detection device, or lighted stylet. (*Note:* Since a misplaced endotracheal tube is a fatal error, there is a trend now for the immediate use of adjuncts to confirm tube placement in every endotracheal intubation.)

The protocol for confirmation of tube placement should be applied immediately following intubation and after several minutes of ventilation. Thereafter the protocol should be followed after movement of the patient from the floor to the stretcher, after loading into the ambulance, and immediately prior to arrival at the hospital. If at any time placement is in doubt, VISUALIZE DIRECTLY OR REMOVE THE TUBE. Never **assume** the tube is in the right place—always be sure and record that the protocol has been carefully followed. Use of CO_2 detectors allows you to maintain continuous monitoring of the tube placement.

Advanced Skill 1F—Anchoring the Tube

This can be a frustrating exercise. Not only does it require some fine movements of the hands when we appear to be all thumbs, but it is difficult to perform this task when ventilation, movement, or extrication is being carried out. There is one thing to keep in mind: There is no substitute for the human anchor. That is, one person should be held responsible for ensuring that the tube is held fast and that it does not migrate in or out of the airway. To lose a tube can be a catastrophe, especially if the patient is inaccessible or the intubation was a difficult one to begin with.

Fixing the endotracheal tube in place is important for several reasons. First, movement of the tube in the trachea will produce more mucosal damage and may increase the risk of postintubation complications. In addition, movement of the tube will stimulate the patient to cough, strain, or both, leading to cardiovascular and intracranial pressure changes that could be detrimental. Most of all, there is a greater risk of dislodging a tube and losing control of the airway if the tube is not anchored solidly in place.

The endotracheal tube can be secured in place by either tape or a commercially available holder. While taping a tube in place is convenient and relatively easily done, it is not always effective, since there is often a problem with the tape sticking to skin that is often wet with rain, blood, airway secretions, or vomitus. If tape is to be used, several principles should be followed:

1. An oropharyngeal airway should also be in place to prevent the patient from biting down on the tube.

2. The patient's face should be dried off and tincture of benzoin applied to better ensure proper adhesion of the tape

3. The tape should be carried right around the patient's neck in anchoring the tube. The neck must not be moved.

4. The tube should be anchored at the labial angle, not in the midline.

Because of the difficulty of fixing the tube in place with tape, we recommend the use of a commercial endotracheal tube holder that uses a small rubber strap to fix the tube in a plastic holder that acts as a bite block. A second rubber strap passes around the patient's neck. While this is not an ideal solution, it is easier to use and more quickly applied. If tube holders with Velcro™ are used, care must be taken not to get the small hooks embedded in the fingers or in the patient's lips.

Since flexion or extension of the patient's head can move the tube in or out of the airway by 2 or 3 cm, it is a good practice to restrict head and neck movement of any patient who has an endotracheal tube in place. If the patient is immobilized because of the risk of cervical spine injury, then you need not worry about this. However, in those who do not have a collar in place, then it is best to tape the head to the backboard or stretcher in order to restrict movement. Failing this, the airway manager is required to ensure that the head and neck are kept in a neutral position.

Advanced Skill 1G—Nasotracheal Intubation

Indications

As with all advanced procedures, this technique must be accepted local protocol and you must have permission from medical direction before performing it.

Indications for performing nasotracheal intubation in the field setting are as follows:

1. A patient who needs endotracheal intubation but who has a possible cervical spine injury

2. A patient who needs endotracheal intubation but who has clenched jaws

3. A patient who needs endotracheal intubation (respiratory distress secondary to large flail chest, open chest wound, blunt trauma to the neck, etc.) but who has a gag reflex

4. A patient who needs endotracheal intubation but who is trapped and you are unable to get into a position to use a laryngoscope

Contraindications

Contraindications to this procedure are as follows:

ABSOLUTE CONTRAINDICATIONS

1. Trauma to the face or nose with possible basilar skull fracture (blood or fluid draining from the nose, facial fractures, and/or raccoon eyes). There is danger of inserting the tube into the cranial vault in this instance.

2. Patients taking anticoagulant medication.

3. Children under the age of ten years

RELATIVE CONTRAINDICATION

It is almost impossible to perform nasotracheal intubation on the patient who is not breathing. You need the sound of the patient's breathing to guide the tube.

Complications

1. Trauma to the nose or airway resulting in hemorrhage and possible aspiration
2. Esophageal intubation leading to hypoxia and death
3. Induction of vomiting, leading to aspiration, hypoxia, and death
4. Right mainstem bronchus intubation
5. Inability to intubate leading to hypoxia and death
6. Trauma to the vocal cords

Equipment

Use the same equipment listed for routine adult endotracheal intubation except modify the adult intubation mannequin by removing one "lung" and attaching a bag-valve device to simulate breath sounds.

Preparation for Intubation

The greatest disadvantage of the nasotracheal route of endotracheal intubation is its relative difficulty, depending as it does on the appreciation of the intensity of the breath sounds of spontaneously breathing patients. It is a blind procedure and as such requires extra effort to demonstrate proper intratracheal placement.

Guidance of the tube through the glottic opening is a question of the intubator perceiving the intensity of the sound of the patient exhaling. The tube can, with some difficulty, be guided toward the point of maximum intensity and slipped through the cords. Breath sounds can be better heard and felt with the ear placed against the proximal opening of the tube or, even better, use of an adjunct such as the Burden nasoscope (see Figure 5-4 in the textbook).

The success of this method will also depend on an anterior curve to the tube that will prevent its passing into the esophagus. This may better be achieved by preparing two tubes prior to carrying out the intubation attempt. The distal end of the 33-cm tube is inserted into its proximal opening, thus molding it into a formed circle. Preparing two tubes permits the immediate use of a second, more rigid tube should the first plastic tube become warm with body temperature, thus losing its anterior curve. Displacing the tongue and jaw forward may also be helpful in achieving placement since this maneuver lifts the epiglottis anteriorly out of the way of the advancing tube.

Procedure

1. Perform routine preparation procedures as described in endotracheal intubation.
2. Following lubrication of its cuff and distal end, a 7.0- or 7.5-mm endotracheal tube with the bevel against the floor or septum of the nasal cavity is slipped distally through the largest naris.
3. When the tube tip reaches the posterior pharyngeal wall, great care must be taken on "rounding the bend" and then directing the tube toward the glottic opening.
4. By watching the neck at the laryngeal prominence, you can judge the approximate placement of the tube. Tenting of the skin on either side of the prominence indicates catching up of the tube in the pyriform fossa, a problem solved by slight withdrawal and rotation of the tube to the midline. Bulging and anterior displacement of the laryngeal prominence usually indicates that the tube has entered the glottic opening and has been correctly placed. At this point the patient, especially if not deeply comatose, will cough, strain, or both. This may be alarming to the novice intubator, who might interpret this as laryngospasm or misplacement of the tube. The tempta-

tion may be to pull the tube and ventilate, since the patient may not breathe immediately. Holding the hand or ear over the opening of the tube to detect air flow may reassure the intubator that the tube is correctly placed, and the cuff may be inflated and ventilation begun.

5. Confirm placement by the confirmation protocol.

BASIC SKILL STATION 2—SPINE MANAGEMENT SKILLS I

Short Backboard and Rapid Extrication

Skill 2A: Spine Management—Short Device

Before beginning, review pages 51–52 in your instructor's guide.

Minimum instructors needed: 1

Objectives

At the conclusion of this station, the student should be able to

1. Explain when to use spinal motion restriction (SMR).
2. Perform SMR with a short device.
3. Perform rapid extrication and emergency rescue.

Important Points

1. The time allowed (30 minutes) to teach this station is very short. You must get started immediately.
2. Most physicians are not taught this skill. It is best to have an experienced EMT teach this station.
3. Do not lecture; demonstrate. Show the students where to put their hands and have them perform the techniques.
4. Weather permitting, this station should be taught outside using a vehicle rather than a chair.

Equipment List

Item	Quantity
Live model	1
Rigid cervical collar	1
Short backboard with straps	1
Long backboard with straps	1
KED or similar vest-type extrication device	1
Head immobilization device	1
Kerlix roll or towels to pad neck	2
Wide adhesive tape	2 rolls
Elastic wraps (ace) 6"	2
Chair or vehicle	1

Procedures

1. Who should receive spinal motion restriction (SMR)?
   a. Any trauma patient with obvious neurological deficit such as paralysis, weakness, or paresthesia (numbness or tingling)

b. Any trauma patient who complains of pain in the neck or back
c. Any trauma patient who is unconscious
d. Any trauma patient who may have injury to the spine but in whom evaluation is difficult due to altered mental status (e.g., drugs, alcohol)
e. Any unconscious patient who may have been subjected to trauma
f. Any patient who has a positive mechanism of injury (see Spinal Trauma chapter in text)
g. When in doubt, use SMR

2. When to use SMR

Patients requiring SMR must be addressed before they are moved at all. In the case of a motor vehicle collision, the patient must receive SMR before being removed from the wreckage. More movement is involved in extrication than at any other time, so SMR must be accomplished before beginning extrication.

3. Technique of SMR using the short device

This device is for use with a patient who is in a position (such as a vehicle) that does not allow use of the long backboard and the patient is not critical. There are several different devices of this type; some devices have different strapping mechanisms from the one explained here. You must become familiar with equipment you will employ before using it in actual patient situations.
a. Remember that the routine priorities of assessment and management are done before the SMR devices go on.
b. One rescuer must, if possible, station himself or herself behind the patient, place his or her hands on either side of the patient's head, and manually maintain the neck in a neutral position. This step is part of the ABCs of assessment. It is done at the same time that you begin assessment of the airway.
c. When you have the patient stable enough to begin SMR, you must apply a rigid cervical collar. If you have enough people, this can be done while someone else is doing the ABCs of assessment and management. If you have limited help, apply the collar after finishing the rapid trauma survey but before transferring the patient to the long backboard.
d. Position the device behind the patient. The first rescuer continues to manually maintain the neck in a neutral position while the short device is being maneuvered into place. The patient may have to be moved forward to get the device in place; great care must be taken so that moves are coordinated to support the neck and back.
e. Secure the patient to the device with the straps that are supplied. Place the short strap under the armpits and across the upper chest as an anchor. Bring each long strap over a leg, down between both legs, back around the outside of the same leg, and then across the chest, and then attach each to the opposite upper strap that was brought across the shoulders.
f. Tighten the straps until the patient is held securely.
g. Secure the patient's head to the device by wide tape or elastic wraps around the forehead. Apply padding under the neck and head as needed to maintain a neutral position.
h. Transfer the patient to a long backboard. Turn the patient so that his or her back is to the opening through which he or she is to be removed. Someone must support the legs so that the upper legs remain at a 90-degree angle to the torso. Position the long backboard through the opening until it is under the patient. Lower the patient back onto the long backboard and slide the patient and the short device up into position on the long backboard. Loosen the straps on the device and allow the patient's legs to extend out flat and then retighten the straps. Now secure the patient to the long board with straps, and secure the head with a padded head device. When the patient is secured in this way, it is possible to turn the whole unit on its side if the patient has to vomit. The patient should remain secure.

Important Points to Remember

1. When you are placing the straps around the legs on a male, do not catch the genitals in the straps.
2. Do not use the short board as a "handle" to move the patient. Move both patient and device as a unit.
3 When you are applying the horizontal strap (long backboard) around a female, place the upper strap above her breasts, not across them.
4. When you are applying the lower horizontal strap on a pregnant patient, see that it is low enough so as not to injure the fetus.
5. You may need to modify how you attach the straps, depending on injuries.
6. Secure the patient well enough so that no motion of the spine will occur if the board is turned on its side. Do not tighten the straps so tight that they interfere with breathing.

Skill 2B—Emergency Rescue and Rapid Extrication

Before beginning, review pages 51–52 in your instructor's guide.

Minimum instructors needed: 1

Objectives

At the conclusion of this station, the student should be able to

1. Explain the indications for emergency rescue and rapid extrication.
2. Demonstrate the techniques of emergency rescue and rapid extrication.

Important Points

1. The time allowed for this station is very short so you must begin immediately.
2. Most physicians are not taught this skill. It is best to assign an experienced EMT to teach this station.

Equipment List

Item	Quantity
Live model	1
Long backboard with straps	1
Rigid cervical collar	1
Head immobilization device	1
Wide adhesive tape	2 rolls
Chair or vehicle	1

Situations Requiring Emergency Rescue or Rapid Extrication

There are two kinds of situations in which you should perform abbreviated extrication. The first of these is an emergency rescue in any situation in which your scene size-up identifies a condition that *immediately* endangers you and your patient. *Immediately* means you may not even have the seconds required to perform an organized rapid extrication and are reduced to simply grabbing and pulling the patient to safety with no regard for spinal precautions. Examples of such situations include

1. Fire or immediate danger of fire
2. Danger of explosion
3. Rapidly rising water
4. Structure in danger of collapse

When performing an emergency rescue, try to drag the patient along the long axis of the body. Above all, get your patient and yourself to safety. Whenever you use this procedure it should be noted in the written report and you should be prepared to explain your actions at a review by your medical direction physician.

The second kind of situation is a rapid extrication in which the initial exam of the patient identifies any condition that requires an *immediate intervention* that cannot be done in the vehicle or other structure. Generally these situations allow you to take the seconds required to do an organized rapid extrication. Examples include

1. Airway obstruction that is not relieved by jaw thrust or finger sweep
2. Cardiac or respiratory arrest
3. Chest or airway injuries requiring ventilation or assisted ventilation
4. Bleeding that cannot be controlled

Rapid extrication is to be used only in a situation where the patient's life is in immediate danger. Whenever you use this procedure it should be noted in the written report and you should be prepared to explain your actions at a review by your medical direction physician.

Procedures

1. One rescuer must, if possible, station himself or herself behind the patient, place his or her hands on either side of the patient's head, and manually maintain the neck in a neutral position. This step is part of the ABCs of assessment. It is done at the same time that you begin assessment of the airway.

2. Do a rapid trauma survey; then apply a cervical collar. You should have the collar with you when you begin.

3. If your rapid trauma survey of the patient reveals an immediate life-threatening situation, go to the rapid extrication technique. This requires at least four, and preferably five or six, rescuers to perform well.

4. Immediately slide the long backboard onto the seat and, if possible, at least slightly under the patient's buttocks.

5. A second rescuer stands close beside the open door of the vehicle and takes over maintaining the cervical spine.

6. Rescuer 1 or another rescuer is positioned on the other side of the front seat ready to rotate the patient's legs around.

7. Another rescuer is positioned at the open door beside the patient. By holding the upper torso, he or she works together with the rescuer, holding the legs to turn the patient carefully.

8. The patient is turned so that his or her back is toward the backboard. The legs are lifted and the back is lowered to the backboard. The neck and back are not allowed to bend during this maneuver.

9. Using teamwork, the patient is carefully slid to the full length of the backboard while the legs are carefully straightened.

10. The patient is then moved immediately away from the vehicle (to the ambulance if available), and resuscitation is begun. The patient is secured to the long backboard as soon as possible.

BASIC SKILL STATION 3—TRACTION SPLINTS

Before beginning, review pages 51–52 in your instructor's guide.

Minimum instructors needed: 1

Objectives

At the conclusion of this station, the student should be able to

1. Explain when to use a traction splint.
2. Describe the possible complications of using a traction splint.
3. Demonstrate how to apply the most common traction splints:
   a. Thomas splint
   b. Hare splint
   c. Sager splint

Important Points

1. The time allowed (30 minutes) is very short. Begin immediately so that each student has time to practice.
2. Most nurses and doctors are not trained in use of traction splints. It is best to assign an experienced EMT to teach this station.
3. Stress when to use traction splints. Make sure the students know that load-and-go patients do not have traction splints applied before transport unless the ambulance has not arrived.
4. You do not have to teach every one of the various traction splints. Teach what is commonly used in your area. There is usually time to practice with at least two types.
5. Do not lecture; demonstrate. Show the students where to put their hands and have them practice the techniques.

Equipment List

Item	Quantity
Thomas splint	1
At least one of the following splints:	
Sager or Hare	
Live models (may use students)	2
Cravats for padding	10
Tongue blades (for Spanish windlass)	10
Adhesive tape (1 inch)	1 roll

Procedures

Traction splints are designed to immobilize fractures of the upper legs. They are useful for fractures of the femur. They are not useful for fractures of the hip, knee, ankle, or foot. Applying firm traction to a fractured or dislocated knee may tear the blood vessels behind the knee. If there appears to be a pelvic fracture, you cannot use a traction splint because it may cause further damage to the pelvis. Fractures below the midthigh that are not angulated or severely shortened may just as well be immobilized by a variety of other splints, such as air splints or the antishock garment. Traction splints work by applying a padded device to the back of the pelvis (ischium) or to the groin. A hitching device is then applied to the ankle and countertraction is applied until the limb is straight and well immobilized. The splints must be applied to the pelvis and groin very carefully to prevent excessive pressure on the genitalia. Care must also be used when attaching the hitching device to the foot and ankle so as not to interfere with circulation. To prevent any unnecessary movement, traction splints should not be applied until the patient is on a long backboard. If the splint extends beyond the end of the backboard, you must be very careful when moving the patient and when closing the ambulance door. You must check the circulation in the injured leg, so remove the shoe before attaching the hitching device. In every case at least two rescuers are needed. One must hold steady, gentle traction on the foot and leg while the other applies the splint. When dealing with load-and-go situations, the splint should not be applied until the patient is in the ambulance and transport has begun (unless the ambulance has not arrived).

A. Thomas Splint (Half-Ring Splint)

1. The first rescuer supports the leg and maintains gentle traction while the second rescuer cuts away the clothing and removes the shoe and sock to check pulse and sensation at the foot.
2. Apply padding to the foot and ankle.
3. Apply the traction hitch around the foot and ankle.
4. Position the splint under the injured leg. The ring goes down and the short side goes to the inside of the leg. Slide the ring snugly up under the hip, where it will be pressed against the ischial tuberosity.
5. Position two support straps above the knee and two below the knee.
6. Attach the top ring strap.
7. Maintain gentle traction by hand.
8. Attach the traction hitch to the end of the splint.
9. Increase traction by Spanish windlass action using a stick or tongue depressors.
10. Release manual traction and reassess circulation and sensation.
11. Support the end of the splint so that there is no pressure on the heel.

B. Hare Splint

1. Position the patient on the backboard or stretcher.
2. The first rescuer supports the leg and maintains gentle traction while the second rescuer cuts away the clothing and removes the shoe and sock to check pulse and sensation at the foot.
3. Apply the padded traction hitch to the ankle and foot.
4. Position the splint under the injured leg. The ring goes down and the short side goes to the inside of the leg. Slide the ring up snugly under the hip against the ischial tuberosity.
5. Position two support straps above the knee and two below the knee.
6. Attach the heel rest.
7. Attach the top strap.
8. Maintain gentle manual traction.
9. Attach the traction hitch to the windlass by way of the S-hook.

10. Turn the ratchet until the correct tension is applied.

11. Release manual traction and recheck circulation and sensation.

12. Attach support straps around the leg with Velcro straps.

13. To release traction, pull the ratchet knob outward and then slowly turn to loosen.

C. Sager Splint

This splint is different in several ways. It works by providing countertraction against the pubic ramus and the ischial tuberosity medial to the shaft of the femur; thus, it does not go under the leg. The hip does not have to be slightly flexed as with the Hare and Thomas. The Sager is lighter and more compact than other traction splints. You can also splint both legs with one splint if needed. The new Sager splints are significantly improved over older models and may represent the state-of-the-art in traction splints.

1. Position the patient on a long backboard or stretcher.

2. The first rescuer supports the leg and maintains gentle traction while the second rescuer cuts away the clothing and removes the shoe and sock to check the pulse and sensation at the foot.

3. Using the uninjured leg as a guide, pull the splint out to the correct length.

4. Position the splint to the inside of the injured leg with the padded bar fitted snugly against the pelvis in the groin. The splint can be used on the outside of the leg, using the strap to maintain traction against the pubis. Be very careful not to catch the genitals under the bar (or strap).

5. While maintaining gentle manual traction, attach the padded hitch to the foot and ankle.

6. Extend the splint until the correct tension is obtained.

7. Release manual traction and recheck circulation and sensation.

8. Apply elastic straps above and below the knee.

BASIC SKILL STATION 4—SPINE MANAGEMENT SKILLS II

Helmet Management—Log-Roll and Long Backboard

Before beginning, review pages 51–52 in your instructor's guide.

Minimum instructors needed: 1

Objectives

At the conclusion of this station, the student should be able to

1. Demonstrate log-rolling a patient onto a long backboard.
2. Demonstrate securing a patient to a long backboard.
3. Demonstrate spinal motion restriction (SMR) for a patient from a standing position.
4. Demonstrate SMR when a neutral position cannot safely be obtained.
5. Explain which patients should have helmets removed in the field and which patients should have helmets stabilized in place.
6. Demonstrate how to remove a helmet properly.
7. Demonstrate proper SMR of a patient who is wearing shoulder pads and a helmet.

Important Points

1. The time allowed (30 minutes) is very short. You must begin immediately.
2. If groups are large enough (6–8), it is best to divide the students into two teams; one to practice log-rolling and helmet management and one to practice securing the patient to the long backboard. You will need a second instructor if you do this.
3. You should review the differences in immobilizing and transporting a pregnant patient.
4. Review the use of padding under the shoulders or torso to maintain a neutral spinal position in children and some elderly patients. It would be useful to have a child or a child mannequin for the students to use in practice.
5. Be sure that students understand that there is some regional variation in who gives the order to roll (rescuer at the head or rescuer at the shoulder). You may use the local preference.
6. The introduction of the vacuum backboard made several of these techniques much easier. You may want to demonstrate this device in this station.

Equipment List

Live model (may use student)	1
Rigid cervical collar	2
Reeve's sleeve (optional)	1
Miller body splint (optional)	1
Vacuum backboard (optional)	1
Long backboard with straps (or strap system)	2
Towels for padding head and neck	4

Cushion-type head immobilizers (optional)	1
Blanket roll	1
Wide adhesive tape	4 rolls
Motorcycle helmet (full face)	1
Football helmet with face protector	1
Shoulder pads	1 set
Open-face helmet	1
Live model	1 or 2

1. Helmet Management

Important Points

1. Patients wearing both shoulder pads and a helmet:
   a. Patients who are wearing both shoulder pads and a helmet will usually have their cervical spines maintained in a more neutral position by leaving the helmet in place and padding and taping the helmet to the backboard to act as a head immobilizer. Football helmets usually fit very snug and make an excellent head immobilizer. They usually raise the head just enough to match the elevation of the shoulders by the shoulder pads. If the face protector must be removed to manage the airway, it can be easily done with scissors or a screwdriver. The team equipment manager has the proper tools to immediately remove face protectors.
   b. If a patient wearing a helmet and shoulder pads has already had the helmet removed when you arrive, or if the helmet must be removed for some reason, you will usually have to place padding under the head to keep the neck in a neutral position.
2. Patients wearing a helmet but no shoulder pads:
   a. Patients with helmets but no shoulder pads will usually have their necks in a flexed position unless the helmet is removed or padding is placed under the shoulders. It is better to remove the helmet.
   b. Motorcycle helmets are usually looser than sports helmets and thus may allow the head to move around inside the helmet. Such helmets do not make good head immobilizers when padded and taped to the backboard.
   c. Because patients come in all shapes and sizes, there may be instances where the patient's neck may be in a more neutral position with the helmet in place. Use judgment in such cases.
   d. Patients who have full-face motorcycle helmets must have the helmet removed in order to assess and manage the airway.

Procedure

1. Divide the students into teams of two to practice helmet removal. Each student should practice at least twice (once as rescuer number 1 and once as rescuer number 2).
2. Review the important points in deciding whether to remove a helmet.
3. Have the students practice padding and taping the helmet of the football player. Also have them practice placing padding under the head of the football player who has already had the helmet removed.
4. Demonstrate how to remove the face protector of a football helmet.
5. Have the students practice removing the motorcycle helmet.

Procedure for Removing a Helmet from a Patient with a Possible Cervical Spine Injury

a. The first rescuer positions himself or herself above or behind the patient, places his or her hands on each side of the helmet, and manually maintains the head and neck by holding the helmet and the patient's neck.

b. The second rescuer positions himself or herself to the side of the patient and removes the chin strap. Chin straps can usually be removed easily without cutting them.

c. The second rescuer then assumes the stabilization by placing one hand under the neck at the occiput and the other hand on the anterior neck with the thumb pressing on one angle of the mandible and the index and middle fingers pressing on the other angle of the mandible.

d. The first rescuer now removes the helmet by pulling out laterally on each side to clear the ears and then up to remove. Football helmets may need to have the air released and ear pads removed. Full-face helmets will have to be tilted back to clear the nose (tilt the helmet, not the head). If the patient is wearing glasses, the first rescuer should remove them through the visual opening before removing the full-face helmet. The second rescuer manually maintains the head and neck during this procedure.

e. After removal of the helmet, the first rescuer takes over SMR by grasping the head on either side with his fingers holding the angle of the jaw and the occiput.

f. The second rescuer now applies a suitable cervical collar.

Alternate Procedure for Removing a Helmet

This procedure has the advantage of one rescuer maintaining immobilization of the neck throughout the whole procedure. This procedure does not work well with full-face helmets.

a. The first rescuer positions himself or herself above or behind the patient and places his or her hands on each side of the neck at the base of the skull. He or she manually maintains the neck in a neutral position. If necessary, he or she may use his thumbs to perform a modified jaw thrust while doing this.

b. The second rescuer positions himself or herself over or to the side of the patient and removes the chin strap.

c. The second EMT now removes the helmet by pulling out laterally on each side to clear the ears and then up to remove. The first rescuer maintains SMR during the procedure.

d. The second rescuer now applies a suitable cervical collar.

Removing a Helmet from a Person Wearing Shoulder Pads

a. Follow usual procedure for removing the helmet.

b. Place towels under head and neck to maintain neutral position.

c. Apply a head device.

2. Log-Rolling the Supine Patient

a. Rescuer 1 maintains SMR. A rigid cervical collar is applied. Even with the collar in place, rescuer 1 maintains the head and neck in a neutral position until the log-rolling maneuver is completed.

b. The patient is placed with legs extended in the normal manner and arms (palms inward) extended by his sides. The patient will be rolled upon one arm with that arm acting as a splint as well as a spacer for the body.

c. The long backboard is positioned next to the patient. If one arm is injured, place the backboard on the injured side so that the patient will roll on the uninjured arm.

d. Rescuers 2 and 3 kneel at the patient's side opposite the board.

e. Rescuer 2 is positioned at the mid-chest area and rescuer 3 is by the upper legs.

f. Rescuer 2, using his or her knees, holds the patient's near arm in place. He or she then reaches across the patient and grasps the shoulder and hips, holding the patient's far arm in place. Usually, it is possible to grasp the patient's clothing to help with the roll.

g. Rescuer 3, with one hand, reaches across the patient and grasps the hip. With the other hand, the feet are held together at the lower legs.

h. Rescuer 2, when everyone is ready, gives the order to roll the patient.

i. Rescuer 1 carefully keeps the head and neck in a neutral position (anterior-posterior as well as laterally) during the roll.

j. Rescuers 2 and 3 roll the patient up on his side toward them. The patient's arms are kept locked to his or her side to maintain a splinting effect. The head, shoulders, and pelvis are kept in line during the roll.

k. When the patient is upon his side, rescuer 2 (or rescuer 4, if available) quickly examines the back for injuries.

l. The long backboard is now positioned next to the patient and held at a 30–45 degree angle by rescuer 4. It there are only three rescuers, the board is pulled into place by rescuer 2 or 3. The board is left flat in this case.

m. When everybody is ready, rescuer 1 gives the order to roll the patient onto the backboard. This is accomplished keeping head, shoulders, and pelvis in line.

3. Log-Rolling the Prone (Face-Down) Patient

The status of the airway is critical for decisions concerning the order of the log-rolling procedure. There are three clinical situations that dictate how you should proceed.

a. The patient who is not breathing or who is in severe respiratory difficulty must be log-rolled immediately in order to manage the airway. Unless the backboard is already positioned, you must log-roll the patient, manage the airway, and then transfer the patient to the backboard (in a second log-rolling step) when ready to transport.

b. The patient with profuse bleeding of the mouth or nose must not be turned to the supine position. Profuse upper airway bleeding in a supine patient is a guarantee of aspiration. This patient will have to be carefully positioned and transported prone or on his or her side, allowing gravity to help keep the airway clear.

c. The patient with an adequate airway and respiration should be log-rolled directly onto a backboard.

The procedure to log-roll the prone patient who has an adequate airway is as follows:

a. Rescuer 1 maintains SMR. When placing the hands on the head and neck, the rescuer's thumbs always point toward the patient's face. This prevents having the rescuer's arms crossed when the patient is rolled. A rigid cervical collar is applied.

b. The rapid trauma survey is done (including the back) and the patient is placed with legs extended in the normal manner and arms (palms inward) extended by his or her side. The patient will be rolled up on one arm, with that arm acting as a splint as well as a spacer for the body.

c. The long backboard is positioned next to the body. The backboard is placed on the side of rescuer 1's lower hand (if rescuer 1's lower hand is on the patient's right side, the backboard is placed on the patient's right side). If the arm next to the backboard is injured, carefully raise the arm above the patient's head so he does not roll on the injured arm.

d. Rescuers 2 and 3 kneel at the patient's side opposite the board.

e. Rescuer 2 is positioned at the midchest area and rescuer 3 is by the upper legs.

f. Rescuer 2 grasps the shoulder and the hip. Usually, it is possible to grasp the patient's clothing to help with the roll.

g. Rescuer 3 grasps the hip (holding the near arm in place) and the lower legs (holding them together).

h. Rescuer 2, when everyone is ready, gives the order to roll the patient.

i. Rescuer 1 carefully keeps the head and neck in a neutral position (anteroposterior as well as laterally) during the roll.

j. Rescuers 2 and 3 roll the patient up on his side away from them. The patient's arms are kept locked to his or her side to maintain a splinting effect. The head, shoulders, and pelvis are kept in line during the roll.

k. The backboard is now positioned next to the patient and held at a 30–45-degree angle by rescuer 4. If there are only three rescuers, the board is pulled into placed by rescuer 2 or 3. The board is left flat in this case.

l. When everyone is ready, rescuer 1 gives the order to roll the patient onto the backboard. This is accomplished keeping the head, shoulders, and pelvis in line.

4. Securing the Patient to the Backboard

There are several different methods of securing the patient using straps. Three of the best commercial devices for SMR are the Reeves sleeve, the Miller body splint, and the vacuum backboard.

The Reeves sleeve is a heavy-duty sleeve into which a standard backboard will slide. Attached to this sleeve are the following:

a. A head device

b. Heavy vinyl-coated nylon panels that go over the chest and abdomen and are secured with heavy nylon straps and quick-release connectors

c. Two full-length leg panels to secure the lower extremities

d. Straps to hold the arms in place

e. Six carrying handles

f. Metal rings (2500-lb strength) for lifting the patient by rope.

When the patient is in this device, SMR is maintained when lifted horizontally, vertically, or even carried on his or her side (like a suitcase). This device is excellent for the confused, combative patient who must be restrained for his own safety.

The Miller body splint is a combination backboard, head device, and SMR device. Like the Reeves sleeve, it does an excellent job of full-body SMR with a minimum of time and effort.

The vacuum backboard, essentially a full-body vacuum splint, actually molds around the patient and can be used to stabilize the head, neck, torso, and extremities in any position. It appears to be an extremely useful piece of equipment.

Many other innovative immobilization devices are now available. Be sure to be familiar with the ones that are in common use in your area.

The procedure for securing the patient to the long backboard using straps is as follows:

a. The head and neck are held in a neutral position (a rigid collar should already be in place) while padding is placed behind the head to maintain this position. A blanket roll or commercial head device is applied and strapped into position using elastic wraps or wide tape. Do not use chin straps unless they can be applied to the chin portion of the cervical collar itself. Chin straps that hold the patient's mouth closed guarantee aspiration if the patient vomits.

b. Two straps are laced through the top two lateral holes of the backboard. Apply them so that they connect together across the chest below the armpits and act as an anchor.

c. Bring the other ends of the straps over the shoulders and across the chest.

d. Lace the straps through the lateral holes at the level of the pelvis.

e. Bring the straps back across the lower pelvis and upper legs, then lace through the lateral holes and connect below the knees. The straps must be applied snugly so that the body does not move if the board has to be turned to allow the patient to vomit.

If you are not using commercial strapping that accompanies the long board, use 12-foot straps. Nine-foot straps will work but are usually too short to go below the knees. If you use two 9-foot straps, most adults will require another strap below the knees.

5. Applying and Securing a Long Backboard to a Standing Patient

Method I

a. One rescuer stands behind the patient and manually maintains the head and neck in a neutral position. A rigid cervical collar is applied. The rescuer continues to maintain SMR.

b. A long backboard is placed on the ground behind the patient.

c. Other rescuers stabilize the shoulders and trunk and allow the patient to carefully sit down on the backboard.

d. The patient is carefully lowered back onto the backboard maintaining stabilization of the head, neck, and trunk.

e. The patient is centered on the backboard and secured.

Method II

a. Rescuer 1 stands in front of the patient and manually maintains the head and neck in a neutral position. A suitable cervical collar is applied. Rescuer 1 continues to maintain SMR.

b. Rescuer 2 places a long backboard against the patient's back.

c. Rescuer 3 secures the patient to the board using straps. These must include an anchor strap high on the chest as well as ones that cross over the shoulders, pelvis, and legs to prevent movement when the board is tilted down.

d. Padding is placed behind the head to maintain a neutral position and a blanket roll or commercial head device is applied and secured using elastic wraps or wide tape.

e. The board is carefully tilted back onto a stretcher.

6. Immobilizing the Head and Neck when a Neutral Position Cannot Safely Be Attained

If the head or neck is held in an angulated position and the patient complains of pain on any attempt to realign it, you should initiate SMR in the position found. The same is true of the unconscious patient whose neck is held to one side and does not easily straighten with gentle traction. You cannot use a cervical collar or commercial head device in this situation. You must use pads or a blanket roll and careful taping to secure the head and neck in the position found.

ADVANCED SKILL STATION 5—CHEST DECOMPRESSION AND FLUID RESUSCITATION

Before beginning, review pages 51–52 in your instructor's guide.

Minimum number of instructors needed: 2

Objectives

At the conclusion of this station, the student should be able to

1. Recite the indications for emergency decompression of a tension pneumothorax.
2. Recite the complications of needle decompression of a tension pneumothorax.
3. Perform needle decompression of a tension pneumothorax.
4. Perform cannulation of the external jugular vein.
5. Recite the indications for use of intraosseous infusion.
6. Perform intraosseous infusion.

Advanced Skill 5A—Chest Decompression

Procedure to Make a One-Way Valve for Decompression

There are several ways to make a one-way valve to attach to the decompressing catheter. The instructor may demonstrate one or all of them.

1. The best valve now available is the Asherman Chest Seal®, which is available commercially and can be used to seal open chest wounds or as a one-way valve for the needle when you decompress a tension pneumothorax (see Figures 6-10 and 6-11).
2. A satisfactory valve can be made by removing the plunger from a plastic 10-cc syringe, cutting the barrel off at about the 5-cc mark, then pulling a penrose drain over the barrel. The device will directly attach to the plastic decompressing catheter and is an excellent one-way flutter valve to allow air to escape (see Figures 6-9, 6-12, 6-13).
3. A water-seal drainage system may be made using a large bore catheter and IV tubing. Cut off the IV tubing where it attaches to the IV bottle. Insert this end into a container of water and place it below the level of the chest. Insert the catheter into the chest and then remove the needle. Attach the IV tubing to the catheter. This is a sophisticated system, although not a practical one, because the container of water is likely to be turned over in a moving ambulance.

Making the Artificial Tension Pneumothorax

Commercial decompressable tension pneumothorax models have been available but they do not work well with the anterior approach. Revised models should be available soon.

Material Needed to Make an Artificial Tension Pneumothorax

1. Section of pork ribs at least 12" by 12"
2. Small trailer wheel inner tube
3. Valve core remover
4. Hand, foot, or electric air pump

5. Two 8-fluid-oz. bottles of tire puncture sealer. The best are Pre-Seal® by Lubri Tech (available at most motorcycle dealers) and Stop-Leak® by Sears (available at any Sears store)

6. Roll of plastic wrap

7. Roll of duct tape or foam latex tape

Procedure to Make the Artificial Tension Pneumothorax

1. Assemble the material.

2. Remove the valve core from the inner tube.

3. Inject the contents of two bottles of tire sealer into the inner tube and replace the valve core.

4. Attach the air pump and pump a small amount of air into the tube.

5. Rotate the tube so that the puncture sealer can coat the entire inner surface.

6. Fold the inner tube over on itself and tape it together with duct tape.

7. Pump up the tube until there is a few pounds of pressure inside. Use just enough to simulate a tension pneumothorax. Excessive pressure will cause the tube to leak when the students begin decompression.

8. Wrap the ribs in plastic wrap.

9. Attach pork ribs over the central area of the tube. Tape well with duct tape or foam latex tape to simulate skin.

10. Use large bore over-the-needle catheter to decompress the "tension pneumothorax".

11. Attach a one-way valve. You can make one from a 10 cc syringe and a penrose drain or use an Asherman Chest Seal®.

12. Occasionally pump more air into the tube to replace the air that has been "decompressed."

Equipment List for Skill Station 5A

Item	Quantity
Artificial tension pneumothorax	1
#14 over-the-needle catheters (Jelco)	20
IV tubing (optional)	1
Small container for water (optional)	1
Rubber condoms (optional)	10
Paper towels (rolls)	1
10 cc syringes	2
Penrose drains	2
Asherman Chest Seal® (optional)	1

Indications

As with all advanced procedures, this technique must be accepted local protocol and you must have permission from medical direction (voice or protocol) before performing. The conservative management of tension pneumothorax is 100 percent oxygen, assisted ventilation, and rapid transport. The indication for performing emergency field decompression is the presence of a tension pneumothorax and more than one of the following:

1. Respiratory distress and cyanosis
2. Loss of the radial pulse (late shock)
3. Decreasing level of consciousness (not from head injury)

Complications

1. Laceration of intercostal vessel with resultant hemorrhage: The intercostal artery and vein run around the inferior margin of each rib. Poor placement of the needle can lacerate one of these vessels.
2. Creation of a pneumothorax may occur if not already present. If your assessment was not correct, you may give the patient a pneumothorax when you insert the needle into the chest.
3. Laceration of the lung is possible. Poor technique or inappropriate insertion (no pneumothorax present) can cause laceration of the lung with subsequent bleeding and more air leak.
4. Risk of infection is a consideration. Adequate skin prep with an antiseptic will usually prevent infection.

Procedure

1. Assess the patient to be sure the condition is due to a tension pneumothorax
   a. Poor ventilation in spite of an open airway
   b. Neck vein distension (may not be present if there is associated severe hemorrhage, i.e., hypovolemic shock)
   c. Tracheal deviation away from the side of the injury (almost never present)
   d. Absent or decreased breath sounds on the affected side
   e. Tympany (hyperresonance) to percussion on the affected side
   f. Shock
2. Give the patient high-flow oxygen and assist ventilation.
3. Determine that indications for emergency decompression are present; then obtain medical direction (protocol or voice) to perform the procedure.
4. Identify the second or third intercostal space on the anterior chest at the midclavicular line on the same side as the pneumothorax. This may be done by feeling the "angle of Louis," the bump located on the sternum about a quarter of the way from the suprasternal notch. The anterior site is preferred because the patient lying supine has a better chance of having accumulated air in the pleural space entered when decompressing at the midclavicular area as opposed to the midaxillary area. Monitoring of the site is also easier if performed in the anterior site because the catheter is not as likely to be unintentionally dislodged when the patient is moved. However, if there is significant anterior chest trauma, the alternate site may be used, the midaxillary line, the fourth or fifth intercostal space directly above the fifth or sixth rib (the nipple is over the fifth rib).
5. Quickly prepare the area with an antiseptic.
6. Use a large bore over-the-needle catheter at least 2 inches (5 cm) long to do the decompression. Remove the plastic cap from the catheter (to allow the air to exit the needle as it passes into the pleural space) and insert the needle into the skin over the superior border of the third rib, midclavicular line. Direct the needle into the intercostal space at a 90-degree angle to the third rib.

The direction of the bevel is irrelevant to successful results. As the needle enters the pleural space, there will be a "pop." If a tension pneumothorax is present, there will be a hiss of air as the pneumothorax is decompressed. Advance the catheter into the chest, remove the needle, and tape the catheter hub to the chest wall.

7. Cover the hub with an Asherman Chest Seal® or attach a one-way valve.

8. Leave the catheter in place until it is replaced by a chest tube at the hospital.

Advanced Skill 5B—Cannulation of the External Jugular Vein

Equipment List

Item	Quantity
Live model	1
Marking pencils (red and blue)	1 each

Important Points

1. Stress the importance of learning to use large bore needles. In the same period of time, a 14-gauge cannula will infuse twice as much fluid as a 16-gauge cannula, and three times as much as an 18-gauge cannula. A 20-gauge cannula infuses so little fluid that it is useful only for pediatric patients or for keep-open lines.

2. Since you are only simulating starting the IV line, you do not actually have to use a needle to demonstrate the technique. Your model will be more comfortable if you use something blunt.

Indication

The pediatric or adult patient who needs IV access and in whom no suitable peripheral vein is found.

Surface Anatomy

The external jugular vein runs in a line from the angle of the jaw to the junction of the medial and middle third of the clavicle. This vein is usually easily visible through the skin and can be made more prominent by pressing on it just above the clavicle. It runs into the subclavian vein.

Procedure

1. The patient must be in the supine position, preferably head down, to distend the vein and prevent air embolism.

2. If there is no danger of cervical spine injury, you should turn the patient's head to the opposite side. If there is a danger of a C-spine injury, one rescuer must stabilize the head in a neutral position (it must not be turned) while the IV is started by a second rescuer.

3. Quickly prepare the skin with an antiseptic and then align the cannula with the vein. The needle will be pointing at the clavicle at about the junction of the middle and medial thirds.

4. With one finger, press on the vein just above the clavicle. This should make the vein more prominent.

5. Insert the needle into the vein at about the midportion and cannulate in the usual way.

6. If it was not already done, draw a 30-cc sample of blood and store it in the appropriate tubes

7. Tape down the line securely. If there is danger of a C-spine injury, a C-collar can be applied over the IV site.

Advanced Skill 5C—Intraosseous Infusion

Equipment List

Item	Quantity
Artificial Infant Leg for IO insertion	2
Betadine solution	4 fluid ounces 10 cc
syringes	1 per student*
16–18-gauge intraosseous needles	1 per student*
Nonsterile rubber gloves	1 box
Paper towels	1 roll

One per student means number of students in the skill station at each teaching session (not the entire class).

Important Points

1. Stress that intraosseous infusion is rarely used as a first line procedure for intravenous access. When it is used in an EMS system, protocols should be employed directing criteria for it to be used.

2. Children, six years of age and younger, are the target population for successful implementation of intraosseous infusion.

3. If you are not going to use one of the commercial pediatric intraosseous legs, the anatomical sites of insertion should be demonstrated using one of the students as a model before practicing on animal bones.

4. Stress that an intraosseous line is never placed in a fractured extremity.

5. As with all advanced procedures, this technique must be accepted local protocol and permission from medical direction (protocol or verbal) must be obtained before performing.

6. If infiltration occurs (rare), do not reuse the same bone. Another site must be selected, as fluid will leak out of the original hole made in the bone.

7. Potential complications:
   a. Subperiosteal infusion due to improper placement
   b. Osteomyelitis
   c. Sepsis
   d. Fat embolism
   e. Marrow damage
   f. Tibial fracture if needle is too large

   Studies have proven all of these complications to be rare; however, good aseptic technique is important, just as with intravenous therapy.

Discussion

The technique of bone marrow infusion of fluid and drugs is not new. Intraosseous infusion (IO) was first described in 1922 and was used commonly in the 1930s and 1940s as an alternative to intravenous infusion of crystalloids, drugs, and blood. The technique was "rediscovered" in the 1980s, and studies have confirmed it to be a fast, safe, and effective route to infuse medications, fluids, and blood.

Intraosseous infusion can be used for giving medications in both adults and children, but because the flow rate is not as rapid as peripheral venous infusions, it cannot be used for rapid volume replacement in adults. Newer techniques such as the F.A.S.T.1™ sternal intraosseous system may prove to offer adequate flow rates for adult volume resuscitation. Intraosseous infusion has the advantage of being quick and simple to perform while providing a stable (anchored in bone) access that is not easily dislodged during transport.

Indications

1. A pediatric or adult patient who is in cardiac arrest and in whom you cannot quickly obtain peripheral venous access
2. Hypovolemic pediatric patients who have a prolonged transport and in whom you are unable to quickly obtain peripheral venous access

Procedure

1. Determine the need for this procedure and obtain permission from medical direction (protocol or verbal).
2. Have all needed equipment ready prior to bone penetration.
3. Identify the site on the proximal tibia, one fingerbreath below the tibial tuberosity either midline or slightly medial to the midline.
4. Prep the skin with antiseptic.
5. Obtain the proper needle. Several commercial IO needles are available. The needle must have a stylet to prevent becoming plugged with bone. While 13-, 18-, and 20-gauge spinal needles will work, they are difficult and uncomfortable to grip during the insertion process. Long spinal needles tend to bend easily, so if you use spinal needles, try to obtain the short ones. The 13-gauge needle can break a bone in a small child so use a smaller needle with smaller patients. The preferred needle is a 14- to 18-gauge intraosseous needle, but bone marrow needles can also be used.
6. Using aseptic technique, insert the needle into the bone marrow cavity. Place sandbags or rolled towels under the knee. Insert the needle (with stylet in place) perpendicular to the skin directed away from the epiphyseal plate and advance to the periosteum. Penetrate the bone with a slow boring or twisting motion until you feel a sudden "give" (decrease in resistance) as the needle enters the marrow cavity. This can be confirmed by removing the stylet and aspirating blood and bone marrow.
7. Confirm proper placement
   a. The needle should stand without support.
   b. You should be able to aspirate bone marrow.
   c. IV fluids should infuse freely.
   For the purposes of this skill station and identification of proper needle placement, have students draw up a small amount of betadine solution and infuse it into the bones to visualize vascular accessibility.
8. Attach standard IV tubing and infuse fluid and/or medications. Tape the tubing to the skin and secure the bone marrow needle as if to secure an impaled object (4 × 4's taped around insertion site).

BASIC SKILL STATION 6—PATIENT ASSESSMENT AND MANAGEMENT

Before beginning, review pages 51–52 in your instructor's guide.

Minimum instructors needed: 1

Objective

At the conclusion of this station, the student should be able to demonstrate the proper sequence of assessment and management of a trauma patient.

Important Points

1. The time allowed (30 minutes) is very short. You must begin immediately.

2. Each group of students will rotate through patient assessment and management twice. Those going through the station the first time should watch you do a demonstration of the BTLS primary survey, detailed exam, and ongoing exam. You should also review the ground rules that will be in effect for the patient assessment scenarios the second day. If time permits have the students practice patient assessment. Those who rotated through the other patient assessment station first should spend the whole period practicing patient assessment. Thus half of the groups will watch you demonstrate assessment and go over ground rules and the other half will spend the period practicing assessment.

3. Every student should be given a grade sheet for study purposes.

4. Students not actually participating in the assessment should follow along with the grade sheet.

5. At the end of the scenario, point out that while this case was a little tricky, it is an example of an actual case in which the patient died because the history of the stab wound was not obtained.

Equipment List (You Will Have Two Stations So Double the Amount Below)

Item		Quantity
Live model		1
Moulage kit or red felt tip pen		1
Rigid cervical collar		1
Monitor-defibrillator (optional)		1
Trauma box (see page 23)		1
BP cuff	1	
Stethoscope	1	
Kerlix rolls	1	
4" elastic wraps	4	
4 × 4 gauze pads (unsterile)	20	
Wide tape (rolls)	1	
IV tubing	2	
Oxygen mask or nasal prongs	1	
Long backboard with straps		1

Cushion-type head immobilizer	1
Asherman Chest Seal®, defibrillation pads, or plastic wrap	1
Grade sheets	1 per student

Procedure

When you are demonstrating assessment, choose two students to assist you perform initial assessment, rapid trauma survey, detailed exam, and ongoing exam. Use the trauma scenario. Explain and demonstrate exactly how you want them to do the exams.

When you are having the students practice patient assessment, select three students to be the rescue team. Have them evaluate the patient who is described in the trauma scenario. Any extra students should follow using the gradesheet. If possible, try to go through the scenario twice so that all the students can participate. If two instructors are present, one instructor should interact with the student during the scenario while the other instructor follows along with the gradesheet (just as you will do in the practice and testing scenarios). The student team leader should be given the completed grade sheet to use for study.

Trauma Scenario

A young male was driving through an intersection. His automobile hit another vehicle. He was not wearing restraints and the vehicle did not have an air bag.

Injuries

1. Fracture of C-7, but no spinal cord injury yet
2. Stab wound to anterior chest with development of pericardial tamponade

Patient Instructions

You are initially awake and alert. If asked, you complain of pain in the left chest and upper back. If your neck is not stabilized or if your neck is allowed to move, immediately become paralyzed.

History

S—pain in left chest and upper back
A—no allergies
M—takes no medications
P—no significant illness
L—last meal eaten two hours ago (hot dogs and lima beans)
E—"I was stabbed by my girlfriend's husband. I was trying to get to the hospital when the accident occurred."

Moulage Instructions

Make contusions over sternum and forehead. Make a small puncture wound on the anterior left chest.

Patient Evaluation: Instructor's Information (Memorize)

Scene Size-Up

No dangers, obvious mechanism of injury is a deceleration automobile accident (windshield cracked, steering wheel bent). The other mechanism is a stab wound of the chest (this must be obtained by history). The driver was the only occupant of his vehicle; the other vehicle had no injured occupants.

Initial assessment

General impression—patient appears in no distress

LOC—patient is alert and responds appropriately

Airway—clear

Breathing—rate: normal, Quality: normal

Ventilation instructions—none, may order oxygen

Circulation:

  Pulse—present and strong at the wrist; rate appears normal

  Bleeding—none obvious

  Skin color and condition—warm and dry and pink

Decision—rapid trauma survey due to mechanism

Rapid Trauma Survey

Head and face—bruising on forehead, otherwise normal

Neck—tender at base of neck, no other signs of trauma.

  Trachea—midline

  Neck veins—flat

Chest—Looking—contusion from steering wheel, small puncture wound to left chest

     Feeling—tender over sternum, no instability, no crepitation

    - Listening—breath sounds present and equal, heart sounds normal

Heart sounds—normal

Abdomen—no DCAP-BTLS

Pelvis—no DCAP-BTLS, no instability or crepitation

Legs—no DCAP-BTLS, no instability or crepitation

Back—no signs of trauma

Decision—load and go due to puncture wound of chest

History (obtained by team leader)—must be given by the patient

  S—Pain in left chest and upper back

  A—No allergies

  M—Takes no medications

  P—No significant illness

  L—Eaten two hours ago (hot dogs and lima beans)

  E—I was stabbed by my girlfriend's husband. I was trying to get to the hospital when the accident occurred

Vital signs (may be obtained by team member)

  BP: 110/70

  Pulse: 90 (slightly irregular)

  Respiration: 20/mm

Decision—Seal puncture wound of chest, give oxygen, start two large bore IVs but run at KVO rate

Detailed exam

History and vital signs: unchanged from above

Neurological

LOC—alert and oriented
Pupils—equal and reactive
Sensory—abnormal "tingling" sensation below the neck
Motor—normal
Head—scalp normal, contusion and tenderness of the forehead, no lacerations or deformity, face—
no DCAP-BTLS, no instability or crepitation, no Battle's sign or raccoon eyes, no blood or
fluid from ears or nose
Airway—open and clear
Breathing—unchanged from above
Neck—tender to palpation
Trachea—midline
Neck veins—slightly distended
Circulation—skin still warm and dry, BP unchanged
Chest—unchanged from above
Heart sounds—normal
Abdomen—no tenderness, not distended
Pelvis—do not examine again
Extremities
Upper—no injuries noted, good pulses and motor function, sensation – some "tingling" feeling
Lower—no injuries noted, good pulses and motor function, sensation – some "tingling" feeling
Decision—continue present treatment
Ongoing exam
Neurological
LOC—patient confused and agitated
Pupils—slightly dilated but react equally
Sensory—unchanged
Motor—unchanged
GCS—(14) eyes (4), verbal (4), motor (6)
Airway—clear
Breathing—rate: 26/minute, quality: normal
Circulation
Pulses—not present at the wrist, present but weak at neck; rate appears rapid
Blood pressure—70/50
Pulse—160/min
Skin color and condition—cool, clammy, and pale
Neck—no swelling or discoloration
Trachea—midline
Neck veins—distended
Chest—Looking—contusion from steering wheel, small puncture wound to left chest
Feeling—no instability, no crepitation
Listening—breaths sounds present and equal, heart sounds decreased from previous
exams
Abdomen—soft, not distended, no response to palpation
Assessment of injuries—no bleeding from the stab wound, no change in bruise on sternum
Interventions:
Transport immediately if not already en route
Check to see that 100 percent oxygen is being given
Begin two IVs if not already done—cautious fluid challenge during transport
Report to medical direction
Cardiac monitor—sinus tachycardia

Pulse oximeter—98 percent saturation
Repeat vital signs after IV fluids:
  BP: 90/60
  Pulse: 130
  Respiration: 24
  Now responds to verbal stimuli

7

Other BTLS Courses

REFRESHER COURSE FOR INSTRUCTORS

Because trauma care changes over time, the BTLS course must change to reflect new standards of care. Instructors who are very active teachers may only require a new textbook and an open-book written test to demonstrate that they understand the changes in the BTLS courses. Most will be better served if they attend a half-day or one-day refresher course to tell them about changes in the book and demonstrate changes in techniques. The following is a tentative agenda for a half-day refresher course. Instructors should read the new edition of the text before the course (unless the course precedes release of a new edition of the text).

Example of a Refresher Course Agenda

Registration and coffee	30 min
Review of the structure of BTLS International and the BTLS chapter structure	15 min
Review of chapter policy and procedures	15 min
Review of new didactic material	60 min
Break	15 min
Demonstration of new skills	60–120 min

RECERTIFICATION COURSE FOR PROVIDERS

Trauma care is changing rapidly, and all professionals experience some degree of skills decay. It is reasonable that every few years BTLS providers should recertify their trauma assessment and management skills. The following is a tentative agenda for a one-day refresher course. Students should reread the book (or read the new edition), take a pretest, and then study the areas identified as weak.

Students should be prepared to take a written test. They will spend the morning reviewing skills and the afternoon reviewing patient assessment.

Example of a Recertification Course Agenda

Registration and collection of pretests	30 min
Written test	60 min
Skill stations	30 min each
Lunch	60 min
Review of patient assessment	15 min
Patient assessment scenario practice and testing	120 min
Faculty meeting	30 min

AFFILIATE FACULTY TRAINING PROGRAM

Instructors who are chosen to be affiliate faculty members should have a brief training session to prepare them for this role. This could be scheduled on the evening before a course in which they are to teach.

Example of an Affiliate Faculty Training Program Agenda

Registration	30 min
Welcome and course overview	5 min
International BTLS: A global perspective	15 min
Chapter BTLS: A local perspective	15 min
Overview of chapter policies and procedures	15 min
Roles and responsibilities of the chapter affiliate faculty	15 min
Common perils and pitfalls encountered in a "typical" BTLS Class	30 min
Review of the BTLS scoring system	5 min
Summary	10 min
Questions and Answers	

BRIDGE COURSE FOR PHTLS INSTRUCTORS

A PHTLS instructor may become a BTLS instructor following successful completion of a chapter-approved bridging course, which emphasizes BTLS patient assessment, administrative structure, and philosophy of BTLS. After completion, the local chapter's policies for provisional instructors will apply and must include monitoring.

Example of a PHTLS to BTLS Instructor Bridge Course Agenda

Registration and collection of pretests   30 min

Written test   60 min

Administrative structure
- BTLS International structure and philosophy
- Chapter structure and philosophy
- Chapter policy and procedures
- Roles of a chapter BTLS instructor
- Chapter precourse and postcourse material   45 min

Break   15 min

Skill stations
- Preskill setup
- Skill lesson presentation
- Assistant instructors   30 min

Instructor candidate demonstrations
- Basic and advanced airway
- Short backboard/KED/rapid extrication
- Traction splints/splinting
- Chest decompression/IV/IO
- Helmet /log-roll/long backboard   90 min

Lunch   60 min

Course objectives, lesson plans, and curriculum   30 min
- Advanced BTLS course lesson plan
- Basic BTLS course lesson plan
- Combined BTLS course lesson plan
- Teaching stations
- Testing stations

BTLS patient assessment   30 min

Patient assessment demonstration   15 min

Instructor candidate demonstrations of   90 min
patient assessment teaching and testing

Faculty meeting

8

Policies and Procedures

Policy and procedure manuals for each chapter are available through that chapter's BTLS office.

THE BTLS ORGANIZATION: BASIC TRAUMA LIFE SUPPORT INTERNATIONAL, INC.

BTLS International, Inc. is a nonprofit corporation for the purpose of providing education to both basic and advanced EMS providers in the management of the acutely traumatized patient.[1] The organization is supported by financial assessments upon every BTLS provider and instructor trained. This assessment was set in place as a voluntary contribution by the chapter organizations at the January 1985 organizational meeting in Atlanta.[2] Other financial support for the organization is provided by royalties from the text and by the sale of texts and accessory materials through the international office.

As stated in the articles of incorporation, the purpose of the organization is to provide trauma training for EMS personnel. However, the proper disposition of the program, including the analysis of methods of education of the adult learner, assessment of the state of the art in trauma care, performance of research in trauma care and patient assessment, efficient management of the organization, provision of venues for organizational meetings, and support of the organization's committees, are clearly issues within the purview of BTLS International.

BTLS International is a continually developing organization. As long as the program is provided as a method of behavior modification relative to patient assessment and management for the EMS provider, BTLS International will continue to exist.

BTLS International, as a nonprofit corporation, has officers and an executive committee. Chapter delegates at the annual meeting of the corporation elect the board of directors annually. The board members have rotating terms of three years, requiring mandatory appraisal by the general body of the organization. Hence, from the most basic provider within the educational framework to the highest tier of organizational management, BTLS is sensitive and responsive to its membership.

The executive director position is occupied by Ginny Kennedy Palys. The board of directors of BTLS appoints this position, and the term is limited only according to regular performance appraisal by the board.

---

[1]BTLS International, Inc., Articles of Incorporation, 1987.
[2]Minutes, BTLS International, January 1985.

International Trauma Conference

Each year the International Trauma Conference is held in a different location throughout the world to facilitate educational sessions and the annual meeting. Opportunity is provided to review the instructional materials, review the results of the program teaching internationally, hear committee reports, and gain general consensus regarding specific items taught within the program, such as how best to perform the patient primary survey in the trauma situation. Representatives from each chapter attend, as well as invited members, such as representatives from ACEP, ENA, and other interested organizations. The BTLS International Trauma Conference meets annually and has done so since January 1985.

CHAPTER STRUCTURE

The educational and business mechanisms of the management of BTLS within a given chapter, are based on two broad groups: the faculty and providers, and the administrative leaders and course managers.

The following levels define the faculty and providers:

Affiliate faculty (also serves as a course manager)
Basic BTLS instructor
Advanced BTLS instructor
Pediatric BTLS instructor
BTLS access instructor
Basic BTLS provider
Advanced BTLS provider
Pediatric BTLS provider
BTLS access provider

The following levels define the administrative leaders of the chapter programs:

Advisory committee member
Advisory committee chair
International meeting delegate
Chapter medical director
Chapter coordinator
International faculty

The following levels define the course managers within the chapter program:

Course medical director
Course coordinator
Affiliate faculty

BTLS ORGANIZATIONAL CHART

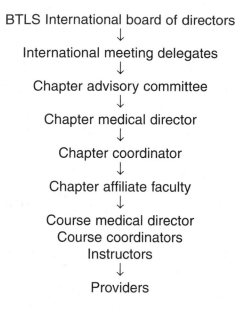

BTLS International board of directors
↓
International meeting delegates
↓
Chapter advisory committee
↓
Chapter medical director
↓
Chapter coordinator
↓
Chapter affiliate faculty
↓
Course medical director
Course coordinators
Instructors
↓
Providers

Responsibilities

The following is a list of some of the ongoing responsibilities of designated BTLS chapters. This list is not all inclusive and may include other chapter-specific responsibilities.

- Coordinate local BTLS courses.
- Collect data, including the number of providers and various faculty members.
- Disseminate information from the BTLS International Office to the constituents of the chapter.
- Provide information to the BTLS International office on BTLS advisory committee activities and new concepts developed within the chapter.
- Provide quality assurance for BTLS courses that are conducted within the chapter.
- Provide local financial management for BTLS chapter programs.
- Provide positive public relations for BTLS advisory committee activities conducted within the chapter.
- Appoint delegates to represent the chapter at the BTLS International Congress.
- Send rosters and fees at least quarterly to BTLS International.

BTLS International Responsibilities to the Chapters

The following is a list of ongoing activities and services that BTLS International provides its chapters. This list is not intended to be all inclusive.

- Disseminate current information to chapters regarding changes in protocols, changes in BTLS teaching materials, and updates on revisions to BTLS International policies and procedures.
- Provide resources to new chapters and organizational materials to assist them in developing BTLS programs.
- Provide a clearinghouse for BTLS international committee recommendations to the chapters.

- Provide quality assurance at an international level by enforcing the guidelines and standards recommended by the BTLS International board of directors and committees.
- Conduct the annual meeting and trauma conference for constituents from all chapters to be represented.
- Prepare financial reports.
- Publish a BTLS International newsletter and maintain a Web site designed to disseminate information to the chapters.
- Distribute BTLS instructional materials and novelties.
- Distribute all BTLS certification cards and certificates, and maintain course roster information.

DESCRIPTION OF BTLS CERTIFICATIONS

Basic BTLS Provider

Prerequisites

The candidate must be an entry-level EMS provider such as a first responder, basic emergency medical technician, or other allied health professional who holds suitable qualifications for entry.

Requirements for Certification

You must attend all the lectures and skill stations and score at least 74 percent on the written test and at least "adequate" on patient assessment. Your chapter may require a higher score.

Length of Certification

Three years or whatever length is deemed appropriate by your chapter.

Recertification

You must attend an approved basic BTLS recertification course prior to the expiration date on the card or complete a certified BTLS provider course. Your chapter may decide which is appropriate.

Advanced BTLS Provider

Prerequisites

The candidate must be an advanced level practitioner such as a certified/licensed EMT–Intermediate, paramedic, registered nurse, physician assistant, physician, or other allied health professional. *(The definition of an advanced level practitioner is one who can perform advanced airway procedures, perform IV cannulation, and administer IV fluids.)*

Requirements for Certification

You must attend all the lectures and skill stations and score at least 74 percent on the written test and at least "adequate" on patient assessment. Your chapter may require a higher score.

Length of Certification

Three years or whatever length is deemed appropriate by your chapter.

Recertification

You must attend an approved advanced BTLS recertification course prior to the expiration date on the card or complete a certified BTLS provider course. Your chapter may decide which is appropriate.

Pediatric BTLS Provider

Prerequisites

It is strongly suggested that the candidate be a certified basic or advanced BTLS or PHTLS provider.

Requirements for Certification

You must attend all the lectures and skill stations and score at least 74 percent on the written test and at least "adequate" on patient assessment. Your chapter may require a higher score.

Length of Certification

Three years or whatever length is deemed appropriate by your chapter.

Recertification

You must attend an approved pediatric BTLS recertification course prior to the expiration date on the card or complete a certified pediatric BTLS provider course. Your chapter may decide which is appropriate.

BTLS Access Provider

Prerequisites

The candidate must be in EMS in at least a first responder role.

Requirements for Course Completion

You must attend the lectures and skill stations. Your chapter may increase these requirements.

Length of Recognition

Three years or whatever length is deemed appropriate by your chapter.

Rerecognition

You must attend an approved BTLS access provider update course.

Basic BTLS Instructor

Prerequisites

Achieve greater than 86 percent on the written test, "excellent" on patient assessment, and be recommended as a potential instructor by an affiliate faculty during a BTLS provider course. The chapter BTLS committee may modify these prerequisites.

Physicians who are board certified in emergency medicine, or are ATLS providers, or who actively participate and teach trauma care may take the instructor course or preceptorship without taking the full provider course.

In unusual circumstances a physician or other EMS provider (EMT, nurse, nurse practitioner, or physician assistant) who has not taken the instructor course may help teach a BTLS course. However, this may be done only with the permission of the chapter BTLS medical director or committee. These requirements are necessary to maintain the high quality of certified courses.

Requirements for Certification

Successful completion of a BTLS Instructor Course or preceptorship and monitoring (in lecture, skills stations, and patient assessment in a provider course) by an affiliate faculty.

Length of Certification

Three years or whatever length is deemed appropriate by the chapter.

Recertification

The instructor must teach at least one BTLS course (instructor or provider) per year for the years of certification. Instructor updates may be required as deemed necessary by the chapter advisory committee. The chapter advisory committee may develop additional criteria.

Removal Procedure

The chapter shall establish a mechanism, through the chapter advisory committee, to revoke the certification of a BTLS basic instructor should the need arise. In addition, the chapter shall establish a method to provide the instructor with due process in the event that the instructor certification is revoked.

> EXAMPLE: If written allegations are made regarding inappropriate conduct by or an inadequate knowledge base of an instructor, the chapter advisory committee may initiate an investigation. The instructor's certification status may also be suspended pending the outcome of the investigation. The chairperson of the chapter advisory committee shall appoint a three-member special committee to conduct the investigation. The investigation shall be completed within 60 days. Upon completion, the instructor will be informed, in writing, of the basis of the allegations and given an opportunity to refute the allegations, in writing, within 30 days.
>
> The special committee will then make recommendations to the chapter advisory committee for action including, but not limited to, one or more of the following:
> a. Temporary suspension of instructor certification for a specified period of time
> b. Permanent suspension of instructor certification
> c. Remedial training
> d. Supervision by an affiliate faculty for a specified period of time

Advanced BTLS Instructor

Achieve greater than 86 percent on the written test, "excellent" on patient assessment, and be recommended as a potential instructor by an affiliate faculty during a BTLS provider course. The chapter advisory committee may modify these prerequisites.

Physicians who are board certified in emergency medicine, or are ATLS providers, or who actively participate and teach trauma care may take the instructor course or preceptorship without taking the full provider course.

In unusual circumstances a physician or other EMS provider (EMT, nurse, nurse practitioner, or physician assistant) who has not taken the instructor course may help teach a BTLS course. However, this may be done only with the permission of the chapter BTLS medical director or committee. These requirements are necessary to maintain the high quality of certified courses.

Requirements for Certification

Successful completion of a BTLS instructor course or preceptorship and monitoring (in lecture, skills stations, and patient assessment in a provider course) by an affiliate faculty.

Length of Certification

Three years or whatever length is deemed appropriate by your chapter.

Recertification

The instructor must teach at least one BTLS course (instructor or provider) per year for the years of certification. Instructor updates may be required as deemed necessary by the chapter advisory committee. The chapter advisory committee may develop additional criteria.

Removal Procedure

The chapter shall establish a mechanism, through the chapter advisory committee, to revoke the certification of an advanced BTLS instructor should the need arise. In addition, the chapter shall establish a method to provide the instructor with due process in the event that the instructor certification is revoked.

> EXAMPLE: If written allegations are made regarding inappropriate conduct by or an inadequate knowledge base of an instructor, the chapter advisory committee may initiate an investigation. The instructor's certification status may also be suspended pending the outcome of the investigation. The chairperson of the chapter advisory committee shall appoint a three-member special committee to conduct the investigation. The investigation shall be completed within 60 days. Upon completion, the instructor will be informed, in writing, of the basis of the allegations and given an opportunity to refute the allegations, in writing, within 30 days.
>
> The special committee will then make recommendations to the chapter advisory committee for action including, but not limited to, one or more of the following:
> a. Temporary suspension of instructor certification for a specified period of time
> b. Permanent suspension of instructor certification
> c. Remedial training
> d. Supervision by an affiliate faculty for a specified period of time

Pediatric BTLS Instructor*

Prerequisites

a. BTLS instructors who pass the pediatric BTLS course may become pediatric BTLS instructors and will only have to be monitored to be certified.

b. Pediatric BTLS students who achieve greater than 86 percent on the written test, "excellent" on pediatric patient assessment, and are recommended as a potential instructor by an affiliate faculty during a pediatric BTLS provider course. The chapter advisory committee may modify these prerequisites.

Requirements for Certification

Successful completion of a BTLS instructor course or preceptorship and monitoring (in lecture, skills stations, and patient assessment in a provider course) by an affiliate faculty. Previous basic or advanced BTLS instructors are not required to take an instructor course or preceptorship and only require monitoring.

Length of Certification

Three years or whatever length is deemed appropriate by your chapter.

Recertification

You must teach at least one pediatric BTLS course per year for the years of certification. Instructor updates may be required as deemed necessary by the advisory committee. The chapter advisory committee may develop additional criteria.

*Basic instructors cannot teach advanced skills or assessment in the Pediatric BTLS Course.

Removal Procedure

The chapter shall establish a mechanism, through the chapter advisory committee, to revoke the certification of a pediatric BTLS instructor should the need arise. In addition, the chapter shall establish a method to provide the instructor with due process in the event that the instructor certification is revoked.

> EXAMPLE: If written allegations are made regarding inappropriate conduct by or an inadequate knowledge base of an instructor, the chapter advisory committee may initiate an investigation. The instructor's certification status may also be suspended pending the outcome of the investigation. The chairperson of the chapter advisory committee shall appoint a three-member special committee to conduct the investigation. The investigation shall be completed within 60 days. Upon completion, the instructor will be informed, in writing, of the basis of the allegations and given an opportunity to refute the allegations, in writing, within 30 days.
> The special committee will then make recommendations to the chapter advisory committee for action including, but not limited to, one or more of the following:
> a. Temporary suspension of instructor certification for a specified period of time
> b. Permanent suspension of instructor certification
> c. Remedial training
> d. Supervision by an affiliate faculty for a specified period of time

BTLS Access Instructor

Prerequisites

Recognized and certified training and experience as an adult educator. Recognized and certified training and experience as a vehicle rescue provider or instructor.

Requirements for Certification

You must be recommended as a potential instructor by an affiliate faculty during a BTLS access course. Becoming a BTLS access instructor is similar to an apprenticeship program. There is no formal course, as the content is completely separate from the usual BTLS core material. The chapter advisory committee may modify these requirements.

Length of Certification

Three years or whatever length is deemed appropriate by your chapter.

Recertification

You must teach at least one BTLS access provider course per year for the years of certification. Instructor updates may be required as deemed necessary by the advisory committee. The chapter advisory committee may develop additional criteria.

Removal Procedure

The chapter shall establish a mechanism, through the chapter advisory committee, to revoke the certification of a BTLS access instructor should the need arise. In addition, the chapter shall establish a method to provide the instructor with due process in the event that the instructor certification is revoked.

> EXAMPLE: If written allegations are made regarding inappropriate conduct by or an inadequate knowledge base of an instructor, the chapter advisory committee may initiate an investigation. The instructor's certification status may also be suspended pending the outcome of the investigation. The chairperson of the chapter advisory committee shall appoint a three-member special committee to conduct the investigation. The investigation shall be completed within 60 days. Upon completion, the instructor will be informed, in writing, of the basis of the allegations and given an opportunity to refute the allegations, in writing, within 30 days.
>
> The special committee will then make recommendations to the chapter advisory committee for action including, but not limited to, one or more of the following:
> a. Temporary suspension of instructor certification for a specified period of time
> b. Permanent suspension of instructor certification
> c. Remedial training
> d. Supervision by an affiliate faculty for a specified period of time

BTLS APPOINTMENTS

Chapter Advisory Committee Member

Duties and Responsibilities

Advise the chapter medical director and chapter coordinator on matters concerning the Chapter BTLS Program on issues such as

- Development of chapter policy and procedures
- Promulgation of BTLS throughout the chapter area
- Development of long-range and strategic plans
- Dissemination of information at the local level
- Disciplinary issues

Other Duties

- Provide input into the process of becoming a chapter.
- Provide mechanism through which personnel throughout the area have a voice in BTLS-related matters.
- Appoint chapter medical director and chapter coordinator.
- In conjunction with the chapter medical director and chapter coordinator, appoint affiliate faculty.
- Oversee the due process of revocation for BTLS instructors, affiliate faculty, course coordinators, and course medical directors.
- Other duties as assigned by the chapter.

Appointed By

The organization holding the charter (for example, in many chapters in the United States, this would be the state's American College of Emergency Physicians [ACEP] chapter).

Length of Appointment

Three years or whatever length is deemed appropriate by the chapter.

Prerequisites

To be set by the organization holding the charter.

> EXAMPLE: Affiliate faculty with extensive knowledge and experience in BTLS and the management of educational programs.

Appointment Process

The advisory committee is first established by the organization holding the charter. They may accomplish this by requesting the appointee's commitment to the evolution of BTLS in the chapter area. A broad base of providers representing all geographical areas should be selected for the committee. Representatives should be basic and advanced EMS providers and other allied health professionals. The chapter developers should invite representation from area emergency medical organizations.

Vacancy Procedure

To be set by the organization holding the charter.

> EXAMPLE: A curriculum vitae (resume), recommendations by two current affiliate faculty, and a letter stating intent should be sent to the chapter advisory committee. The advisory committee shall select the most suited for the position from the pool of applicants.

Reappointment Procedure

To be set by the organization holding the charter.

> EXAMPLE: The performance of the advisory committee members will be subject to review to determine the advisability of reappointment. The review will be completed by the entity or organi-

zation that appointed the member with recommendation by the chapter medical director. The review will be held on a schedule consistent with the length of term of the committee. It is suggested that one third of members be reviewed annually.

Removal

The chapter shall establish a mechanism, through the entity or organization that appointed the chapter advisory committee, to remove the designation of a chapter advisory committee member should the need arise. In addition, the chapter shall establish a method to provide the chapter advisory committee member with due process in the event that the designation is revoked.

> EXAMPLE: If written allegations are made regarding inappropriate conduct by or an inadequate knowledge base of the chapter advisory committee member, the entity or organization that appointed the chapter advisory committee may initiate an investigation. The chapter advisory committee member designation may also be suspended pending the outcome of the investigation. The entity or organization that appointed the chapter advisory committee member shall appoint a three-member special committee to conduct the investigation. The investigation shall be completed within 60 days. Upon completion, the chapter advisory committee member will be informed, in writing, of the basis of the allegations and given an opportunity to refute the allegations, in writing, within 30 days.
>
> The special committee will then make recommendations for action including, but not limited to, one or more of the following:
> a. Temporary suspension of the chapter advisory committee member designation for a specified period of time
> b. Permanent suspension of chapter advisory committee member designation
> c. Remedial training
> d. Supervision by the chapter advisory committee and/or chapter coordinator

Advisory Committee Chairperson

Duties and Responsibilities

- Lead and supervise the BTLS committee.
- Serve as the liaison between the BTLS advisory committee and the charter holder.
- Advise the organization holding the charter board of directors on issues relative to the operation of the BTLS program and the progress of the committee.
- Oversee the operation of the BTLS advisory committee.
- Appoint ad hoc subcommittees as needed to address specific BTLS issues.
- Provide leadership for the BTLS advisory committee for strategic and long-range planning.
- Appoint a special committee to execute due process in the event of revocation.
- Other duties as assigned by the chapter.

Appointed By

The organization holding the charter.

Length of Appointment

One year or whatever length is deemed appropriate by the chapter.

Prerequisites

- Must be a member of the advisory committee.
- The nominee should have extensive experience in managing continuing education courses and demonstrate an in-depth knowledge of BTLS.
- Experience as a committee chairperson is preferred.

Appointment Procedure

Set by the organization holding the charter.

> EXAMPLE: The BTLS advisory committee chairperson will be appointed by the BTLS charter holder from the body of the BTLS advisory committee.

Reappointment Procedure:

Set by the organization holding the charter.

> EXAMPLE: The performance of the committee chairperson should be reviewed on an annual basis by the medical director, peer review, and/or the charter holder's board of directors to determine the advocacy of reappointment. Should the chairperson not demonstrate satisfactory performance or not wish to continue, the charter holder's board of directors shall ask for his or her resignation and initiate a search for qualified candidates.

Removal

The chapter shall establish a mechanism, through the entity or organization that appointed the chapter advisory committee chairperson, to remove the designation of a chapter advisory committee chairperson should the need arise. In addition, the chapter shall establish a method to provide the chapter advisory committee chairperson with due process in the event that the designation is revoked.

> EXAMPLE: If written allegations are made regarding inappropriate conduct by or an inadequate knowledge base of the chapter advisory committee chairperson, the entity or organization that appointed the chapter advisory committee may initiate an investigation. The chapter advisory committee chairperson designation may also be suspended pending the outcome of the investigation. The entity or organization that appointed the chapter advisory committee chairperson shall appoint a three-member special committee to conduct the investigation. The investigation shall be completed within 60 days. Upon completion, the chapter advisory committee chairperson will be informed, in writing, of the basis of the allegations and given an opportunity to refute the allegations, in writing, within 30 days.
>   The special committee will then make recommendations for action including, but not limited to, one or more of the following:
> a. Temporary suspension of the chapter advisory committee chairperson designation for a specified period of time
> b. Permanent suspension of chapter advisory committee chairperson designation
> c. Remedial training
> d. Supervision by the chapter advisory committee and/or chapter coordinator

International Faculty

BTLS International sponsors an annual meeting and conference for trauma education and for conducting business and elections for the BTLS International board of directors. The number of votes a chapter is awarded for the business session of the International conference is determined by the number of BTLS certifications issued during the past two calendar years. In order for these certifications to be valid, payment and rosters must be submitted prior to March 31 of the next year. It is the prerogative of the chapter BTLS advisory committee to appoint International faculty to represent accurately the interests of the chapter.

Duties and Responsibilities

- Represent the BTLS chapter as an International meeting delegate.
- Communicate the perspective of the chapter with regard to major issues.
- Disseminate information to all members of the advisory committee as required.
- Participate in the assessment of the BTLS program.
- Participate in the formative process of continuing course revision.
- Participate in the development of BTLS International, Inc.

Prerequisites

- Should be affiliate faculty
- Should have a strong working knowledge of BTLS and related issues
- Orientation by the chapter medical director and/or the advisory committee to the position

Appointed By

BTLS advisory committee and/or the chapter medical director.

Length of Appointment

Duration of the annual international meeting or whatever length is deemed appropriate by the chapter.

Chapter Medical Director

Duties and Responsibilities

- Ultimately responsible for the management of the BTLS program within the chapter, in both educational and business-related matters.
- Provide consistent leadership for the program.
- Stimulate the evolution and consistency of BTLS programs throughout the chapter area.
- Ensure the availability of training and the quality of the programs offered.
- Ensure the medical appropriateness of the course content.
- Ensure that the program is taught in a manner consistent with the EMS laws of the chapter.
- Ensure the medical quality of BTLS courses throughout the chapter.
- Advise the chapter BTLS advisory committee on the appointments of affiliate faculty.

- Represent BTLS as an International meeting delegate, if possible.
- Regularly review the courses held under the auspices of the appointed course directors within the chapter.
- Relieve a course director of this title if he or she fails to present courses that are consistent with BTLS standards, or where management of the course impedes student education or the reputation of the chapter BTLS program.
- Relieve a course coordinator of this title if he or she fails to present courses that are consistent with BTLS standards, or where management of the course impedes student education or the reputation of the chapter BTLS program.
- In association with the chapter coordinator, facilitate the daily operation of the BTLS program.
- Oversee the appeal of due process activities.
- Other duties as assigned by the chapter.

Prerequisites

- Must be a physician licensed to practice medicine within the chapter area plus other criteria developed by the chapter

  EXAMPLES:

  - Should be a physician involved in emergency medicine with a background of involvement in prehospital care
  - Should be a BTLS Instructor

Appointed By

BTLS advisory committee and/or the sponsoring organization holding the charter.

Length of Appointment

Two years or whatever length is deemed appropriate by the chapter. The performance of the director should be reviewed on an annual basis to determine the advocacy of reappointment.

Removal

The chapter shall establish a mechanism, through the entity or organization that appointed the chapter medical director, to remove the designation of a chapter medical director should the need arise. In addition, the chapter shall establish a method to provide the chapter medical director with due process in the event that the designation is revoked.

EXAMPLE: If written allegations are made regarding inappropriate conduct by or an inadequate knowledge base of the chapter medical director, the chapter advisory committee may initiate an investigation. The chapter medical director's designation may also be suspended pending the outcome of the investigation. The entity or organization that appointed the chapter medical director shall appoint a three-member special committee to conduct the investigation. The investigation shall be completed within 60 days. Upon completion, the chapter medical director will be informed, in writing, of the basis of the allegations and given an opportunity to refute the allegations, in writing, within 30 days.

The special committee will then make recommendations for action including, but not limited to, one or more of the following:

a. Temporary suspension of the chapter medical director designation for a specified period of time
b. Permanent suspension of chapter medical director designation
c. Remedial training
d. Supervision by the chapter advisory committee and/or chapter coordinator

Chapter Coordinator

Duties and Responsibilities

- In association with chapter medical director, facilitate the daily operation of the BTLS program.
- Provide consistent leadership for the program.
- Stimulate the evolution and consistency of BTLS programs throughout the chapter area.
- Ensure the availability of training and the quality of the programs offered.
- Provide financial management and oversight of the BTLS chapter, including organization of chapter finances.
- Ensure the quality and consistency of BTLS, focusing primarily on the administrative aspects.
- Advise the chapter advisory committee regarding the appointment of affiliate faculty.
- Represent BTLS as an International meeting delegate.
- Organize chapter records.
- Provide administrative support for the BTLS chapter.
- Execute the plans and enforce the policies of the BTLS Policy and Procedure Manual.
- Coordinate due process activities of the chapter advisory committee.
- Other duties as assigned by the chapter.

Prerequisites

- Must possess and maintain affiliate faculty status or be the administrative designate of the BTLS chapter
- Should be an individual who has experience in managing continuing education courses and has demonstrated an in-depth knowledge of prehospital and hospital trauma care
- Other criteria as determined by the chapter

Appointed By

BTLS advisory committee and/or the sponsoring organization holding the charter.

EXAMPLE: The chapter coordinator is elected by the BTLS advisory committee and serves a two-year term or whatever is deemed appropriate by the chapter. The performance of the coordinator should be reviewed on an annual basis to determine the advocacy of reappointment. Should the coordinator not demonstrate satisfactory performance or not wish to continue, the BTLS advisory committee shall initiate a search for a qualified candidate.

Length of Appointment

Two years or whatever length is deemed appropriate by the chapter.

Removal

The chapter shall establish a mechanism, through the entity or organization that appointed the chapter coordinator, to remove the designation of a chapter coordinator should the need arise. In addition, the chapter shall establish a method to provide chapter coordinator with due process in the event that the designation is revoked.

EXAMPLE: If written allegations are made regarding inappropriate conduct by or an inadequate knowledge base of chapter coordinator, the chapter advisory committee may initiate an investigation. The chapter coordinator designation may also be suspended pending the outcome of the investigation. The entity or organization that appointed the chapter coordinator shall appoint a three-member special committee to conduct the investigation. The investigation shall be completed within 60 days. Upon completion, the chapter coordinator will be informed, in writing, of the basis of the allegations and given an opportunity to refute the allegations, in writing, within 30 days.

The special committee will then make recommendations for action including, but not limited to, one or more of the following:

a. Temporary suspension of the chapter coordinator designation for a specified period of time
b. Permanent suspension of chapter coordinator designation
c. Remedial training
d. Supervision by the chapter medical director and/or chapter advisory committee

Affiliate Faculty

Duties and Responsibilities

- Monitor the quality of BTLS courses in the chapter.
- Serve as a resource person for course medical directors and course coordinators.
- Monitor new BTLS instructors.
- Participate as faculty for instructor courses and updates.
- Participate as faculty for provider courses.
- Participate in the BTLS advisory committee structure.

EXAMPLES:

- Serve as the primary liaison between BTLS instructors and the BTLS advisory committee.
- Disseminate information to providers and instructors.
- Promote BTLS.
- Provide valuable input affecting decisions made at the chapter level.
- Other duties as assigned by the chapter

Prerequisites

- Must keep BTLS instructor certification current
- Should complete a chapter BTLS advisory committee approved affiliate faculty training program

- Must possess considerable knowledge with respect to the BTLS chapter structure and operations
- Must be willing to maintain active involvement with the development of BTLS educational material
- Must possess a willingness to promote actively the growth and development of the BTLS program
- Other criteria as assigned by your chapter

Appointed By

BTLS advisory committee and/or chapter medical director. Affiliate faculty should be equally distributed throughout the chapter.

> EXAMPLE OF APPOINTMENT PROCEDURE: A curriculum vitae (resume), recommendations by two current affiliate faculty, and a letter stating intent should be sent to the chapter advisory committee. The advisory committee shall vote on the appropriateness of the appointment.
>
> EXAMPLE OF REAPPOINTMENT PROCEDURE: Reappointment of affiliate faculty should be determined by their yearly activities which should include participation in at least two BTLS courses per year and/or on the needs and demands of the chapter. Reappointment is not considered an automatic right or due.

Length of Appointment

Twelve months or whatever length is deemed appropriate by the chapter.

Removal

The chapter shall establish a mechanism, through the chapter advisory committee, to revoke the affiliate faculty designation of a BTLS (basic, advanced, or pediatric) instructor should the need arise. In addition, the chapter shall establish a method to provide the affiliate faculty member with due process in the event that the designation is revoked.

> EXAMPLE: If written allegations are made regarding inappropriate conduct by or an inadequate knowledge base of the affiliate faculty member, the chapter advisory committee may initiate an investigation. The affiliate faculty member's designation may also be suspended pending the outcome of the investigation. The chairperson of the chapter advisory committee shall appoint a three-member special committee to conduct the investigation. The investigation shall be completed within 60 days. Upon completion, the affiliate faculty member will be informed, in writing, of the basis of the allegations and given an opportunity to refute the allegations, in writing, within 30 days.
>
> The special committee will then make recommendations to the chapter advisory committee for action including, but not limited to, one or more of the following:
> a. Temporary suspension of the affiliate faculty designation for a specified period of time
> b. Permanent suspension of affiliate faculty designation
> c. Remedial training
> d. Supervision by the chapter medical director and/or chapter coordinator

Course Medical Director

Duties and Responsibilities

- Provide clinical oversight during the course.
- Act as a resource to the affiliate faculty members present.
- Promote professional relationship with EMS providers during the course.
- In the absence of an instructor, be prepared to present information.
- Chair faculty meetings.
- Must be in attendance at advanced courses (length of time required to be present at the course is determined by the chapter). The chapter may choose to make the course medical director's on-site presence a requirement for all provider courses. When present the course medical director may lecture and is encouraged to participate in all course sessions, including practical skills and patient assessment stations. When not present during the course, the medical director should be available by phone for consult with affiliate faculty members.

Prerequisites

- The course medical director must be a licensed physician within the chapter boundaries.
- Should be familiar with EMS systems and prehospital care and have experience and training related to trauma patients.
- Should be a BTLS instructor or should serve as co-director for one course with a physician BTLS instructor.
- If not a BTLS instructor, must be familiar with the BTLS curriculum, particularly the patient assessment component.

Approved By

The chapter medical director.

Length of Appointment

The time frame of the scheduled BTLS course.

Removal

The chapter shall establish a mechanism, through the chapter advisory committee, to remove the designation of a course medical director should the need arise. In addition, the chapter shall establish a method to provide the course medical director with due process in the event that the designation is revoked.

> EXAMPLE: If written allegations are made regarding inappropriate conduct by or an inadequate knowledge base of the course medical director, the chapter advisory committee may initiate an investigation. The course medical director's designation may also be suspended pending the outcome of the investigation. The chairperson of the chapter advisory committee shall appoint a three-member special committee to conduct the investigation. The investigation shall be completed within 60 days. Upon completion, the course medical director will be informed, in writing, of the basis of the allegations and given an opportunity to refute the allegations, in writing, within 30 days.

The special committee will then make recommendations to the chapter advisory committee for action including, but not limited to, one or more of the following:

a. Temporary suspension of the course medical director designation for a specified period of time
b. Permanent suspension of course medical director designation
c. Remedial training
d. Supervision by the chapter medical director and/or chapter coordinator

Course Coordinator

Duties and Responsibilities

- Must be present throughout the course and will serve as the primary resource for information and questions of an administrative nature.
- Coordinate all aspects of the BTLS course:
  - proper precourse preparation
  - ordering of textbooks
  - ordering and distribution of BTLS educational resources to students and lecturers
  - arranging for equipment
  - on-site coordination, including meals and breaks
  - registration of students
  - appropriate placement of equipment in working order
  - flow of skills stations
  - patient assessment practice and testing stations
  - grading of written exams
  - submission of the appropriate paperwork and fees to the chapter office within required time frame
- The course coordinator must work closely with the course medical director, affiliate faculty, and BTLS chapter office
- Other duties as assigned by the chapter.

Prerequisites

- BTLS certification preferred but not required.
- Experienced EMS educator and program organizer with thorough knowledge of the BTLS program. A demonstrated history of coordinating and conducting multiple session programs (e.g. ACLS, PALS, etc.) is helpful.
- Able to coordinate all requirements precourse, during the course, and postcourse follow-up.
- These prerequisites may be modified by the chapter.

Appointed By

The chapter coordinator.

Removal

The chapter shall establish a mechanism, through the chapter advisory committee, to remove the designation of a course coordinator should the need arise. In addition, the chapter shall establish a method to provide the course coordinator with due process in the event that the designation is revoked.

> EXAMPLE: If written allegations are made regarding inappropriate conduct by or an inadequate knowledge base of the course coordinator, the chapter advisory committee may initiate an investigation. The course coordinator's designation may also be suspended pending the outcome of the investigation. The chairperson of the chapter advisory committee shall appoint a three-member special committee to conduct the investigation. The investigation shall be completed within 60 days. Upon completion, the course coordinator will be informed, in writing, of the basis of the allegations and given an opportunity to refute the allegations, in writing, within 30 days.
>
> The special committee will then make recommendations to the chapter advisory committee for action including, but not limited to, one or more of the following:
> a. Temporary suspension of the course coordinator designation for a specified period of time
> b. Permanent suspension of course coordinator designation
> c. Remedial training
> d. Supervision by the chapter medical director and/or chapter coordinator

MISCELLANEOUS POLICIES

Certification Cards

Students who pass a certified BTLS course should get their cards at the end of the course. At no time should they have to wait longer than 90 days after a course to get their cards.

BTLS Reciprocity with PHTLS

A PHTLS instructor may become a BTLS instructor following successful completion of a chapter-approved bridging course that emphasizes BTLS patient assessment, the administrative structure, and philosophy of BTLS. After completion, the local chapter's policies for provisional instructors will apply and must include monitoring.

A PHTLS provider may become a BTLS provider by taking and passing a BTLS provider course.

BTLS Instructor Reciprocity with Chapters

Instructor certification will be accepted from any other chapter. An instructor coming into a different BTLS chapter must apply to the BTLS chapter coordinator for reciprocity. This application will include the instructor's past activities regarding BTLS teaching and a letter confirming good standing from his or her former chapter medical director.

Once approved by the BTLS chapter coordinator, the instructor must be monitored while teaching by a chapter affiliate faculty. Upon completion of monitoring, the affiliate faculty will send his or her recommendation to the BTLS chapter coordinator. The chapter coordinator may issue a certification card or, in the case of an unfavorable recommendation, present the results to the chapter advisory committee.

BTLS Provider Reciprocity with Chapters

BTLS providers from other chapters will be accepted to the date of expiration of their certification card. The provider must attend a BTLS course within the chapter to recertify. The chapter may modify this requirement.

Teaching Certified Courses in Areas that Do Not Have a Chapter

Certified BTLS courses to be taught in areas that do not have a BTLS chapter must be cleared through the Global Development Committee. This can be accomplished by calling BTLS International at 1-800-495-BTLS (outside U.S.: 630-495-6442).

Medical Director Involvement in BTLS Courses

To be certified, a BTLS course must be taught by registered BTLS instructors under the sponsorship of BTLS International. The course does not certify future performance, nor does it confer license of any kind on successful completion.

BTLS International strongly recommends on-site involvement of physician instructors in BTLS courses to integrate material into the local emergency medical service systems, as well as to provide medical oversight.

Each course must have a medical director who is available for consultation during the course. The course medical director acknowledges accountability by being familiar with all course content and ensuring that the course is taught per guidelines of the chapter's policy and procedures and BTLS International.

When the course medical director is not on site, each course must have a designated affiliate faculty who is on site and accepts responsibility for overall quality assurance.

The participation of both the course medical director and affiliate faculty provide the necessary quality assurance, overall responsibility, and adherence to BTLS International standards.

*Check local chapter policy.

Bridge Course Policy

In an effort to facilitate the process by which certified trauma instructors may become BTLS instructors, BTLS has developed a bridge course. The following policy outlines the course requirements. BTLS chapters may modify the policy as needed for their specific needs.

This course is open to any currently certified PHTLS or ATLS instructor who wishes to become a BTLS Instructor. A BTLS faculty member must conduct the course.

- Rationale: This course has been developed to facilitate the process by which certified trauma instructors may become certified as BTLS instructors. The course assumes that the candidate is familiar with basic instructional methodology and the skills of BTLS. Successful completion certifies the candidate as a BTLS instructor candidate.

- Necessary prerequisites: The prerequisite for registering in the bridge course is current PHTLS or ATLS (or similar trauma training program) instructor certification.

- Certified by: Following completion of the bridge course, the candidate is classified as an instructor candidate. To become certified as a BTLS instructor, the candidate must be recommended for certification by a faculty member who monitors the candidate teaching during a BTLS provider course. Monitoring must be within 12 months of the bridge course and include teaching a lecture and a skill station. An extension may be granted for the 12 months if considered appropriate by the chapter medical director.

- Certified for: Three years.
- Recertification: To be recertified as a BTLS instructor, the individual must teach and be monitored in at least one BTLS course (basic or provider) per year for the three years of certification. Instructor updates may be required as deemed necessary by the chapter.
- Recommended course length: One day.
- Required text: BTLS instructor manual and BTLS provider manual.

9

Makeup Techniques

The purpose of makeup or moulage is to help the student's assessment by making the patient situation more realistic. The students will get the feel of an emergency situation more easily if the patient has injuries that appear genuine. Beautiful but delicate makeup is often destroyed before the first group is through their practice; thus, you must use judgment in applying makeup. Many injuries or signs of injury (distended neck veins, deviated trachea, sucking chest wound, flail chest) can be shown better (and longer) by simply writing on a piece of white tape and sticking it to the skin in the appropriate place. If the student examines the patient and sees "distended neck veins" and "trachea deviated to the right" written on the tape, the effect is better than having to ask the instructor or having to guess what smudged or "fallen off" moulage once represented. Makeup is probably best used to simulate cyanosis or shock, bruising, lacerations, burns, or abrasions. Having an experienced makeup artist prepare the models is preferable, but with a little knowledge and practice, the average person can do a surprisingly good job.

Selection of Models

Treatment of the multiple trauma patient requires exposure of the injured areas, including the chest, so less embarrassment is involved if most of the models are male (the pregnant patient, of course, is best portrayed by a female). Warn all models (especially female) to wear bathing suits under their clothes.

If the "patients" have some knowledge of the symptoms pertaining to their "injuries," it will add to the realism. EMTs and nurses often make the best "patients," and it is a learning experience for them. The faculty in each station should discuss with the model exactly how to portray his injuries. If you choose to do moulage, allow a minimum of two hours for model preparation.

Makeup Kit

A wound simulation kit is commercially available. It contains artificial blood, other makeup materials, and various plastic or rubber simulated injuries to be attached to the skin. You can assemble your own makeup kit at considerable savings. The following lists include many of the items necessary. Almost all of the material can be found at local hardware, grocery, or drug stores

Item	Quantity
Isopropyl alcohol	1 bottle
Vaseline®	1 jar
Paper towels	2 rolls
KY jelly®	2 tubes
Cold cream	1 jar
Small hair dryer	1
Facial tissues	1 box
Glycerin	1 bottle
Spray bottle	2
Assorted sponges (to apply makeup)	
Saran Wrap®	1 roll
Rubber condoms	6
Red, blue, and black felt-tip pens	1 each
Can of waterless hand cleaner	1
Alka-Seltzer tablets®	1 small bottle
Makeup colors: maroon, red, white, blue, brown, yellow, flesh	
Artificial blood (theatrical supply)	1 pack
Plumber's putty (get at hardware store; it takes the place of mortician's wax)	1 can
Duo® surgical adhesive (theatrical supply)	1 bottle
Grease stick, black	1
Activated charcoal	1 small container
Irrigation bulb (to apply charcoal)	1
Tongue depressors (to mold putty)	1 box
Toothpicks (to mold putty)	1 box
Soft and stiff bristled artist brushes	1 each
Scissors	1 pair
Rubber gloves (unsterile)	1 box

Additional Material

    Pieces of bone (from baked chicken or turkey).
    Black blood (for the depths of wounds)—mix charcoal, white petrolatum, and blood powder.
    Coagulated blood—mix KY jelly and powdered blood.
    Regular blood—mix stay-flo liquid starch and food coloring or powdered blood.
    Sweat (diaphoresis)—mix two parts glycerin and one part water. Use in spray bottle.
    Ashes
    Dirt
    Pieces of broken clear plastic or Plexiglas

Skin Preparation

Where makeup is to be applied, first apply a thin layer of cold cream. This is very important for makeup removal later. In areas where wounds are to be attached (glued prostheses or molded putty), clean the skin of all oil and grease with a paper towel and alcohol.

Wound Simulation

Applying makeup color is better done with rubber gloves or the small sponges than with your bare fingers. When using putty, use a tongue blade and toothpick to smooth and shape.

1. *Shock.* Use white makeup. Apply a *small* amount to the center of the forehead and each cheek. Smooth it out uniformly until the skin has a pale appearance. Do not apply the makeup too heavily or the model will look like a clown.

2. *Cyanosis.* Use medium blue makeup. Apply a tiny amount to the nose, lips, earlobes, and fingernails. It is best to use this in conjunction with the "shock" makeup.

3. *Diaphoresis.* Mix two parts glycerin and one part water in a spray bottle. Spray it on the patient just before the student begins evaluation. Keep out of patient's eyes—it burns.

4. *Blood.* Simulated blood is used in wounds and on clothing to give a dramatic effect. You will need blood of regular consistency, "clotted" blood, and "black" blood. Be very careful when using artificial blood, because it stains carpet and even some tile. Place a plastic sheet under the patient to prevent the blood from coming into contact with tile or carpet.

5. *Burns.* Cover the area with a thin layer of red or maroon makeup. Do not smooth it out uniformly; burns are not uniform. Now scatter several "blisters" of Vaseline scattered over the area. Cover this with Saran Wrap or facial tissue and press it down. You will have very realistic blisters where the Saran Wrap covers the globs of Vaseline. Facial tissue can be torn to look like broken blisters. Apply black grease paint around the edges of the Saran Wrap. Spray the area with a small amount of the glycerin–water mixture and apply a thin layer of ashes, which should cover the edges well and give a uniform appearance. Don burned clothing.

6. *Basilar skull fracture.* Put a few drops of blood in either ear. Allow a small amount to trickle down the face. Apply black makeup around eyes to simulate "raccoon eyes."

7. *Abrasions.* Apply maroon liner to the area with a makeup brush or sponge. Smooth and thin the edges so they blend into the skin. Cover the wound with a thick layer of Duo surgical adhesive and dry with hair dryer. When it is dry, pick and tear the center of the adhesive to resemble sloughed, abraded skin. Rub a small amount of maroon and red cream over and under the adhesive layer. Apply a small amount of glycerin and then clotted blood. Dirt also adds a realistic touch.

8. *Contusions.* Since bruises are usually raised in the center, it is best to use an area of bony prominence for bruises. Apply red and maroon cream, mixed together. Thin the outside edge in an irregular manner. Use a brush to apply blue liner to the outer one-third of the red-maroon area. Do not blend in completely. It should have a mottled appearance.

9. *Lacerations.* First clean the skin well with alcohol. With plumber's putty fashion a thin layer (1/8-inch thick at the thickest part) on the clean skin. Feather the edges. Use the edge of the tongue blade to make a gash across the putty. Use flesh-colored makeup over the entire area and the surrounding skin to blend the putty and skin. Apply black blood to the depth of the wound. Mix clotted blood and ashes and dab the mixture on the area. Then pour a small amount of blood into the gash and allow it to trickle down.

10. *Sucking chest wound.* Clean the skin with alcohol. Apply putty with one-half of an Alka-Seltzer tablet embedded in it. Feather the edges and make a hole in the putty to resemble a penetrating wound. Apply maroon or red makeup. Dab on a mixture of blood and ashes. Now make a hole down to the Alka-Seltzer tablet. Just before the student comes in, pour a small amount of artificial blood down the hole onto the tablet. It will bubble like a sucking chest wound.

11. *Penetrating object.* This wound is simulated with the same technique as lacerations and sucking chest wounds. Use enough putty to secure the penetrating object. Do not use heavy objects (they will pull the putty loose) or sharp objects (they may cause real lacerations). Use plastic not glass.

12. *Protruding intestines.* You may use the commercial moulage for this or make very realistic intestines from two rubber condoms filled with KY jelly. The ends are tied off and they are wrapped around each other to simulate loops of intestines. Vascular markings are made with the red and blue felt-tip pens. Attach these to the skin and apply clotted and regular artificial blood.

13. *Open fractures.* Commercial moulage is best for this, but if you must, apply and blend putty to the area. Incise the putty with a toothpick or tongue blade, then apply makeup to simulate bruised and torn flesh. Use black blood in the base of the wound, and then add bone fragments (small) and clotted blood.

Clothing

A good source of old clothing (other than your closet) is the Salvation Army or Goodwill store. They usually have some clothing in poor condition, which can be purchased for very little cost. Get the largest sizes available. If you plan to teach courses regularly, it is best to cut the clothing at the seams and sew in velcro strips so the clothing can be "ripped open" for exam of the patient and then stuck back together for the next group.

STUDENTS' GUIDE TO BTLS

BTLS Mission Statement

BTLS is a global organization dedicated to preventing death and disability from trauma through education about emergency trauma care and trauma prevention.

What to Wear at the Course

BTLS is a practical course that stresses hands-on teaching. You should wear comfortable clothes that you do not mind getting dirty. Blue jeans and sweatshirts are perfect.

How to Prepare for the Course

You absolutely must read and study the BTLS book before the course. There is not enough time in two days to learn the written material, the skills, and imprint the BTLS patient assessment method. The philosophy of a two-day hands-on course is to be familiar with the material beforehand, to review the concepts briefly, and then to spend most of the time practicing the practical applications of those concepts. The best method of preparation is to

1. Read the book through once (including skill stations that are to be taught in your course—you should be notified if you are to be responsible for any of the optional skills). Unless notified in writing, you are not required to read nor will you be tested on material in the appendix.
2. Take the pretest.
3. Reread the book, paying particular attention to those subjects identified as weaknesses by the pretest.
4. Memorize the initial exam, rapid trauma survey, detailed exam, and ongoing exam.
5. If possible, practice patient assessment using the team approach as outlined in Chapter 3.

Grades

If you are taking a certified course, you will have to take a written exam and a practical test. The practical test is patient assessment. You will not be required to test on each of the skills taught in the skill stations. However, you will be required to use those skills correctly in the management of your simulated patients. The written test is composed of 50 questions and requires a grade of at least 74 percent to pass. Patient assessment is a practical exam, and you are graded on your overall management of the problem. Some students with superior performance may be asked to become instructor candidates.

Schedule

You will be sent a schedule for the course. BTLS is a very intensive learning course, and time must be used efficiently. You must be familiar with your skill station schedule so that you have time to practice each skill during the brief time available.

How to Function as a Team

1. Decide who will be the team leader, Rescuer 2, and Rescuer 3. Change each time you practice so that each member gets to be team leader once.
2. Before entering the room, be sure each of you understands your duties.

Team Leader

You are responsible for the overall performance of the team. You must direct other team members to do certain actions if they do not do them on their own. You must perform the scene size-up, see that the spine is stabilized, and perform the patient assessment. You are the only member who should directly interact with the instructor. The other team members report to you and you are responsible for their actions. You should help carry some of the equipment to the patient.

Rescuer 2

While the team leader is sizing up the scene, you should get the cervical collar, trauma box, and oxygen equipment and carry it to the patient. Do not approach the patient until the team leader states that it is safe to do so. When you approach the patient you will place the equipment within easy reach and immediately stabilize the patient's cervical spine (unless the team leader elects to do this). You must maintain stabilization of the neck with either your hands or your knees until the patient is transferred to a backboard and the head immobilizer is applied. You are also in charge of maintaining the airway and appropriate ventilation. The team leader should give you ventilation instructions as soon as the airway has been examined. If the team leader forgets to give you instructions, you may ask, "Are there any ventilation instructions?"

Rescuer 3

While the team leader is surveying the scene, you should get the backboard and head immobilizer and be ready to place them next to the patient. You should assist with helmet removal, stop bleeding, dress wounds, and proceed with other tasks as delegated. You should help transfer the patient to the backboard and secure the straps. Team members do *not* have to stand around waiting to be told to do something, but they must *not* take over the evaluation of the patient. The team leader may elect to stabilize the neck but is still responsible for assessing the patient and assuring that all procedures are performed. This is accomplished more easily if Rescuer 2 is allowed to maintain stabilization.

Review Ground Rules for Teaching and Testing and Patient Assessment Pearls on pages 47–49 of the BTLS text (advanced and basic).

OPTIONAL SKILL STATIONS

OPTIONAL SKILL 1—ANTISHOCK GARMENT APPLICATION

Before beginning, read pages 51–52 in your instructor's guide.

Minimum instructors needed: 1

Objectives

At the conclusion of this station, the student should be able to

1. Recite the indications and contraindications for the use of the antishock garment.
2. Apply and inflate the antishock garment.
3. Deflate and remove the antishock garment.

Equipment List

Item	Quantity
Extrication dummy (you may use a Resusci-Annie or a live model). If you use a Resusci-Annie, you must use pediatric size MAST. If you use a live model, you should only simulate inflating the garment.	2
Blood pressure cuff	2
Stethoscope	2
Long backboard	1
Traction splint	1
Antishock garments (MAST, PASG)	2

Indications for Use on the Antishock Garment in Trauma Patients

1. Shock secondary to hemorrhage that can be controlled
2. Neurogenic shock without evidence of other internal injuries
3. Isolated fractures of legs without evidence of other internal injuries (blow up to only air-splint pressures)
4. Systolic blood pressure less than 50 mm Hg (controversial)

Contraindications for Use of Antishock Garment

1. Absolute:
   a. Pulmonary edema
   b. Bleeding that cannot be controlled, such as penetrating chest or abdominal trauma
2. Conditional: pregnancy—may use leg compartments

Procedure

APPLICATION

a. Evaluate the patient through at least the BTLS rapid trauma survey. Apply a blood pressure cuff to the arm.

b. Have the second rescuer unfold the trousers and lay them flat on a long backboard and place the backboard beside the patient.

c. Maintaining immobility of the spine, log-roll the patient (check the back quickly as you do this) onto the backboard. The top of the antishock garment should be just below the ribs.

d. Wrap the trousers around the left leg and fasten the Velcro strips.

e. Wrap the trousers around the right leg and fasten the Velcro strips.

f. Wrap the abdominal compartment around the abdomen and fasten the Velcro strips. Be sure the top of the garment is below the bottom ribs.

g. Attach the air tubes from the foot pump to the connections on the trousers.

INFLATION OF TROUSERS

a. Recheck and record the vital signs.

b. Inflate the leg compartments while monitoring the blood pressure. If the systolic blood pressure is not in the range 90 to 100 mm Hg, inflate the abdominal compartment.

c. When the patient's blood pressure is adequate (90 to 100 mg Hg), turn the stopcocks to hold the pressure.

d. Remember: It is not the pressure in the trousers you are monitoring but the pressure in the patient.

e. Continue monitoring the patient's blood pressure, adding pressure to the trousers as needed.

DEFLATION OF TROUSERS

Note: Before deflation occurs, two large-bore IVs must be inserted and sufficient volume of fluids and/or blood given to replace the volume lost from hemorrhage. The antishock garment is usually deflated only at the hospital. The only reason to deflate them in the field is if they cause difficulty with breathing (pulmonary edema).

a. Record the patient's vital signs.

b. Obtain permission to deflate the trousers from a physician knowledgeable in their use.

c. Slowly deflate the abdominal compartment while monitoring the patient's blood pressure.

d. If the blood pressure drops 5 mm Hg or more, you must stop deflation and infuse more fluid or blood until the vital signs stabilize again (this usually requires at least 200 cc).

e. Proceed from the abdominal compartment to the right leg and then left leg with your deflation, continuously monitoring the blood pressure and stopping to infuse fluid when a drop of 5 mm Hg occurs.

f. If the patient experiences a sudden precipitous drop in blood pressure while you are deflating, stop and reinflate the garment.

APPLICATION OF ANTISHOCK GARMENT TO A PATIENT REQUIRING A TRACTION SPLINT

a. Have your partner hold traction on the fractured leg.

b. Unfold the trousers and lay them flat on a long backboard.

c. Log-roll the patient, holding traction on the injured leg and keeping the neck stabilized.

d. Slide the backboard and the patient so that the top of the trousers is just below the lowest rib. If the patient is already on a backboard, you may simply unfold the trousers and slide them under the patient while maintaining traction on the injured leg.

e. Wrap the trousers around the injured leg and fasten the Velcro strips.

f. Wrap the trousers around the other leg and fasten the Velcro strips.

g. Wrap the abdominal compartment around the abdomen and fasten the Velcro strips. Be sure that the top of the garment is below the bottom ribs.

h. Apply a traction splint (Thomas, Hare, or Sager) over the trousers. Attach the straps and apply traction.

i. Inflate the trousers in the usual sequence.

OPTIONAL SKILL 2—DIGITAL INTUBATION

Before beginning, review pages 51–52 in your instructor's guide.

Minimum instructors needed: 1

Objectives

At the conclusion of this skill station, the student should be able to

1. Recite the indications for digital intubation.
2. Perform digital intubation.

The original method of endotracheal intubation, widely known in the eighteenth century, was the tactile or digital technique. The intubator merely felt the epiglottis with the fingers and slipped the endotracheal tube distally through the glottic opening. Recently the technique has been refined and demonstrated to be of use in the prehospital setting for a wide variety of patients.

Indications

Tactile orotracheal intubation is particularly useful for deeply comatose or cardiac arrest patients who

1. Are difficult to position properly
2. Are somewhat inaccessible to the full view of the rescuer
3. May be at risk of cervical spine injury
4. Have facial injuries that distort anatomy
5. Have copious oropharyngeal bleeding or secretions that impair visualization of the airway

Personnel may prefer to perform tactile intubation when they are more confident in their ability with this technique, or when a laryngoscope fails or is not immediately available. We have found the technique most valuable in those patients in difficult positions (e.g., extrications) and in those who have copious secretions despite adequate attempts at suctioning.

Equipment

This method of intubation requires the following:

1. An endotracheal tube, 7.0, 7.5, or 8.0 mm internal diameter
2. A malleable stylet (note: some prefer to perform the procedure without a stylet)
3. A water soluble lubricant (use silicone spray for mannequin)
4. A 12-cc syringe
5. A dental prod, mouth gag, or something similar for placing between the teeth
6. Rubber examining gloves
7. Adult intubation mannequin

Procedure

1. Perform routine preparation procedures as described for endotracheal intubation.
2. The tube is prepared by inserting the lubricated stylet and bending the tube into an "open J" configuration. The stylet should not protrude beyond the tip of the tube, but it should come to at least the side hole.
3. A water-soluble lubricant is used liberally on the tip and cuff of the tube.
4. The intubator kneels at the patient's left shoulder facing the patient and places a dental prod or mouth gag between the patient's molars.
5. The intubator then "walks" the index and middle fingers of his left hand down the midline of the tongue, all the while pulling forward on the tongue and jaw. *This is an important maneuver and serves to lift the epiglottis up within reach of the probing fingers.*
6. The middle finger palpates the epiglottis. It feels much like the tragus of the ear.
7. The epiglottis is pressed forward and the tube is slipped into the mouth at the left labial angle anterior to the palpating fingers. The index finger is used to keep the tube tip against the side of the middle finger (that is still palpating the epiglottis). This guides the tip to the epiglottis. The side hole of the tube can also be used as a landmark to ensure that the intubator is always aware of the position of the tip of the endotracheal tube. *This is a crucial principle of this technique.*
8. Guide the tube tip to lie against the epiglottis using the middle and index fingers. The right hand then advances the tube distally through the cords as the index and middle fingers of the left palpating hand press forward to prevent the tube from slipping posteriorly into the esophagus. *Note:* At this point the tube/stylet combination may encounter resistance, especially if the distal curve of the tube is sharp. This usually means that the tube tip is pressing on the anterior wall of the thyroid cartilage. Pulling back slightly on the stylet will allow the tube to conform to the anatomy, and the tube should slip into the trachea.
9. Confirm placement by the confirmation protocol taught in Chapter 5 (advanced text).

OPTIONAL SKILL 3—TRANSILLUMINATION (LIGHTED STYLET)

Before beginning, review pages 51–52 in your instructor's guide.

Minimum instructors needed: 1

Objective

Upon completion of this station, the student should be able to perform endotracheal intubation by the transillumination method.

The transillumination or lighted stylet method of endotracheal intubation is based on the fact that a bright light inserted inside the upper airway can be seen through the soft tissues of the neck when inside the larynx or trachea. This permits the intubator to guide the tube tip through the glottic opening without directly visualizing the cords. It has been called the indirect visual method and has been shown in several studies to be reliable, quick, and atraumatic. It is particularly attractive in trauma patients since it appears to move the head and neck less than conventional orotracheal methods.

Equipment

1. Stylet—the lighted stylet is a malleable wire connecting a proximal battery housing to a distal light bulb and covered with a tough plastic coating that prevents the light from being separated from the wire. The wire stylet part is 25 cm in length. An on/off switch is located at the proximal end of the battery housing.

2. Endotracheal tubes—all tubes should be 7.5 to 8.5 mm internal diameter and should be cut to 25 cm to accommodate the stylet.

3. Other equipment is the same as listed for orotracheal intubation.

Important Points

The success of this method of intubation will depend on several factors:

1. The level of ambient light
2. Pulling forward on the patient's tongue, or tongue and jaw
3. The bend of the tube-stylet

The light should be cut down to about 10 percent of normal, or the neck should be shielded from direct sun or bright daylight. While the transilluminated light can be perceived in thin patients even in daylight, success will be more likely in darker surroundings.

Pulling forward on the tongue (or tongue and jaw) lifts the epiglottis up out of the way. This is essential to this method.

The stylet/tube combination should be bent just proximal to the cuff. A bend that is too far proximal will cause the tube to strike against the posterior pharyngeal wall and prevent the tube advancing anteriorly through the glottic opening. The lubricated stylet is slipped into the tube and held firmly against the battery housings while the tube-stylet is bent. Bend more sharply if the patient is not in the sniffing position.

Procedure

1. Perform routine preparation procedures as described in Chapter 5.

2. The intubator stands or kneels on either side facing the patient's head. Gloves are worn for the procedure. The light is turned on.

3. The patient's tongue (or, more easily, the tongue and jaw) is grasped by the intubator and drawn gently forward while the liberally lubricated tube-stylet combination is slipped down the tongue.

4. Using a "soup ladle" motion, the epiglottis is "hooked up" by the tube-stylet and the transilluminated light can be seen in the midline. Correct placement at or beyond the cords is indicated by the appearance of a circumscribed, easily perceived light at the level of the laryngeal prominence. A dull glow, diffuse and difficult to see, indicates esophageal placement.

5. When the light is seen, the stylet is held firmly in place and the fingers of the other hand support the tube lying along the tongue as they advance the tube off the stylet more distally into the larynx.

6. Confirm placement of the tube with the confirmation protocol as described in Chapter 5.

OPTIONAL SKILL 4—ESOPHAGEAL GASTRIC TUBE AIRWAY

Before beginning, review pages 51–52 in your instructor's guide.

Minimum instructors needed: 1

Objectives

At the conclusion of this station, the student should be able to

1. Explain the seven essential points about the use of this airway.
2. Correctly insert the esophageal gastric tube airway (EGTA.)

Equipment List

Item	Quantity
Adult intubation mannequins	2
EGTAs	2
9-mm cuffed ET tubes	2
Can of silicone lubricant spray	2
35-cc syringes	2
Oral airways (size to fit adult mannequin)	2
Tonsil suctions tip (Yaunker) and suction tubing	2 each
Bag-valve devices	2
Nonsterile rubber gloves	1 box
Face shields or goggles	2

Several essentials must be remembered about the use of the EGTA:

1. It is used only for patients who are unresponsive and without protective reflexes.
2. It should *not* be used for patients with upper airway or facial trauma where bleeding into the oropharynx is a problem. It must *not* be used in any patient with injury to the esophagus (e.g., caustic ingestions) or in children who are under the age of 15 and are of average height and weight.
3. Adequate mask seal must be ensured; this means appropriate lifting forward of the jaw, with careful attention to keeping the neck immobile.
4. Great attention must be paid to proper placement. Unrecognized intratracheal placement is a lethal complication that produces complete airway obstruction. Such an occurrence is not always easy to detect, and the results are catastrophic. One of the great disadvantages of this airway is the fact that correct placement can be determined only by auscultation and observation of chest movement—both may be quite unreliable in the prehospital setting.
5. Insertion must be gentle and without force.
6. The EGTA should not be removed from an unconscious patient without first inserting an endotracheal tube to protect the airway. Patients almost always vomit when the EGTA is removed.

7. The EGTA is not recommended in place of the endotracheal tube but rather can be used for patients in whom attempts at endotracheal intubation have been unsuccessful. Even in these, careful attempts at intubation should be continued despite the successful insertion of an EGTA.

Note: Demonstrate how to replace the EGTA tube with a #9 ET tube. The 15 mm adapter will fit in the same hole as the EGTA tube adapter (it may require some trimming). The #9 ET tube is approximately the same size and length as the EGTA tube and it will tolerate being inflated with 35 cc of air. There are several advantages of using the ET tube with the EGTA. The larger hole in the ET tube makes suctioning easier, it is less expensive to replace the ET tube than to replace the entire EGTA, and you can remove the face mask and ventilate directly through the ET tube if you inadvertently intubate the trachea while inserting the EGTA.

Procedure

The airway is relatively easily inserted and must never be forced. In the supine patient the following procedure is used:

1. Ventilation should be carried out with mouth-to-mask or bag-valve-mask and suctioning performed prior to insertion of the airway.
2. After liberal lubrication, the airway, with mask attached, is slid into the oropharynx while the tongue and jaw are pulled forward.
3. The airway is advanced along the tongue and into the esophagus. Care should be taken to observe the neck. "Tenting" of the skin in the area of the pyriform fossa, or anterior displacement of the laryngeal prominence indicates that misplacement has occurred. The airway should be repositioned by pulling back and reinserting.
4. Following gentle insertion (without force) so that the mask now rests easily on the face, the mask is sealed firmly on the face as the jaw is pulled forward to ensure a patent airway.
5. Prior to inflating the cuff, ventilation is attempted with mouth-to-mask or bag-valve device. If the chest is seen to rise, breath sounds are heard, and compliance appears good, the cuff of the airway is inflated with 35 cc of air.
6. Following inflation, the lung fields are auscultated again and the chest wall is felt as well as observed for movement. The epigastrium should not distend.

If there is any doubt about the placement of the airway, remove it and reinsert. If the patient regains consciousness, you must remove the EGTA. Extubation is likely to cause vomiting; be prepared to suction the pharynx and turn the backboard.

OPTIONAL SKILL 5—TRANSLARYNGEAL JET VENTILATION

Before beginning, review pages 51–52 in your instructor's guide.

Minimum instructors needed: 1

Objective

Upon completion of this station, the student should be able to perform translaryngeal jet ventilation.

Important Points

When access below the level of the cords is sought, translaryngeal jet ventilation (TLJV) provides a quick, reliable, and relatively safe method of adequate oxygenation and ventilation, especially in the trauma patient. Many misconceptions and erroneous impressions persist about this technique, and the medical literature is confusing on the subject. Clinical experience and studies done using appropriate equipment in both animals and patients would clearly indicate the following:

1. Patients can be both oxygenated and ventilated with this technique that delivers 100 percent oxygen in volumes exceeding one liter per second.
2. Ventilation can proceed indefinitely, provided the correct size cannula is used with the proper driving pressure.
3. Cannulae of 14 gauge or larger, with side holes, must be used.
4. Driving pressures of at least 50 psi must be used to deliver sufficient volumes to ensure adequate ventilation.

Patients cannot be ventilated using small-bore cannulae with continuous flow oxygen attached: The forgoing principles must be adhered to if this technique is to be used safely and effectively.

Equipment

The tools needed for TLJV should be prepared well in advance and stored in a small bag or kit:

1. A #14 or #13 gauge cannula, with side holes—these sizes are the minimum necessary for adequate ventilation. Side holes are especially important, since they prevent the cannula from remaining against the tracheal wall and subjecting it to sudden pressures that could rupture it.
2. A manual jet ventilator device—these are commercially available and are merely valves that allow high-pressure oxygen to flow through them when a button is pushed. They should have high-pressure tubing attached solidly with special fasteners and tape.
3. Wrench—a small wrench should be attached to the jet ventilator tubing so that no time will be lost looking for a way to tap into the oxygen tank, or turn it on.
4. Cricoid stick mannequin.

Procedure

Identification of the cricothyroid membrane is essential to this technique, although placement between the tracheal rings would probably not result in major complications.

1. While continuing attempts at ventilation and oxygenation, the cricothyroid membrane is punctured by the cannula firmly attached to a 5-cc syringe filled with 1 or 2 cc of saline. Several milliliters of 2 percent lidocaine can be used instead of saline, to produce local anesthesia of the mucosa in the area of the distal port of the cannula.

2. The cannula is directed downward, with continual aspiration to promptly demonstrate entry into the larynx, identified when bubbles of air are readily aspirated. At this point, if lidocaine is contained in the syringe, it can be injected to provide some anesthesia and prevent the coughing that sometimes occurs in those patients who are somewhat responsive.

3. On entry into the larynx, the cannula is slid off the needle trochar and is held in place while the TLJV is connected to the proximal port of the cannula.

4. The patient is immediately ventilated using one-second bursts of oxygen from the 50-psi manual source. The rate used is at least 20/minute (i.e., an inspiratory/expiratory ratio of 1 : 2).

5. If a tie is available, the cannula is fixed in place. Tape can also be used, but it must be fastened firmly to the cannula and then around the patient's neck. Firm pressure at the site of insertion can reduce the small amount of subcutaneous emphysema that usually occurs with this technique.

OPTIONAL SKILL 6—PHARYNGO-TRACHEAL LUMEN AIRWAY

Before beginning, review pages 51–52 in your instructor's guide.

Minimum instructors needed: 1

Objectives

Upon completion of this skill station, the student should be able to

1. Explain the five essential points about use of this airway.
2. Correctly insert the pharyngo-tracheal lumen airway (PtL®).

Important Points

The pharyngo-tracheal lumen airway is another airway developed for EMS providers who are not trained to perform endotracheal intubation. The PtL consists of a smaller-diameter long tube inside of a short, large-diameter tube. The longer tube goes either into the trachea or the esophagus, while the shorter tube opens into the lower pharynx. Each tube has a cuff; the longer tube's cuff seals the esophagus or trachea, and the shorter tube's cuff seals the oropharynx so that there is no air leak when you ventilate the patient. You insert the PtL blindly into the pharynx and then you must carefully determine whether the longer tube is in the esophagus or the trachea. If the long tube is in the trachea, you ventilate through it. If the tube is in the esophagus, you ventilate through the larger tube in the pharynx. The PtL has advantages over the EGTA in that you don't require extra hands to keep a seal with a face mask and also the cuff in the pharynx prevents blood and mucus from entering the airway from above.

You must remember five essential points about the PtL:

1. Use only in patients who are unresponsive and without protective reflexes.
2. Do not use in any patient with an injury to the esophagus (e.g., caustic ingestions) or in children who are under the age of 15 and are of average height and weight.
3. Pay careful attention to proper placement. Unrecognized intratracheal placement of the long lube is a lethal complication that produces complete airway obstruction. Such an occurrence is not always easy to detect, and the results are catastrophic. Like the EGTA, one of the great disadvantages of this airway is the fact that you can determine correct placement only by auscultation and observation of chest movement. Both may be unreliable in the prehospital setting.
4. You must insert gently and without force.
5. If the patient regains consciousness, you must remove the PtL as it will cause retching and vomiting.

Equipment List

Item	Quantity
Adult intubation mannequins	2
PtL airways	2
Cans of silicone lubricant spray	2
35-cc syringes	2

Tonsil suctions tip (Yaunker) and suction tubing	2
Bag-valve devices	2
Nonsterile rubber gloves	1 box
Face shields or goggles	2

Procedure

The airway is relatively easily inserted and must never be forced. In the supine patient, the following procedure is used:

1. Ventilate with mouth-to-mask or bag-valve-mask and suction the pharynx prior to insertion of the airway.

2. Prepare the airway by checking to be sure that both cuffs are fully deflated, that the long #3 tube has a bend in the middle, and that the white cap is securely in place over the deflation port located under the #1 inflation valve.

3. After liberal lubrication, slide the airway into the oropharynx while the tongue and jaw are pulled forward.

4. Holding the PtL in your free hand so that it curves in the same direction as the natural curvature of the pharynx, advance the airway behind the tongue until the teeth strap contacts the lips and teeth. On very small patients you may have to withdraw the airway so that the teeth strap is up to an inch from the teeth. Conversely, on very large patients you may have to insert the teeth strap into the mouth, past the teeth.

5. Immediately inflate both cuffs. Make sure that the white cap is in place over the deflation port located under the inflation valve. Deliver a sustained ventilation into the inflation valve. You can detect failure of the cuffs to inflate properly by failure of the external pilot balloon to inflate or by hearing or feeling air escape for the patient's mouth and nose. This usually means that one of the cuffs is torn and the airway must be removed and replaced. When you determine that the cuffs are inflating, continue inflation until you get a good seal.

6. Immediately determine whether the long #3 tube is in the esophagus or the trachea. First ventilate through the short #2 tube. If you see the chest rise, hear breath sounds, feel good compliance, and hear no breath sounds over the epigastrium, the long #3 tube is in the esophagus and you should continue ventilating through the #2 tube.

7. If you do not see the chest rise, hear breath sounds, and feel good compliance when the #2 tube is ventilated, the #3 tube is probably in the trachea. In this case, remove the stylet from the #3 tube and ventilate through the #3 tube. If you see the chest rise, hear breath sounds, feel good compliance, and hear no breath sounds over the epigastrium, the #3 tube is in the trachea and you should continue ventilating through the #3 tube.

8. When you are sure that the patient is being adequately ventilated, carry the neck strap over the patient's head and tighten it in place. Continually monitor the appearance of the pilot balloon during ventilation. Loss of pressure in the balloon signals a loss of pressure in the cuffs. If you suspect a cuff is leaking, increase pressure by blowing into the #1 inflation valve or replace the airway.

Like the EGTA, if the patient becomes conscious, you must remove the PtL. Remove the white cap from the deflation port to simultaneously deflate both cuffs. Extubation is likely to cause vomiting; be prepared to suction the pharynx and turn the backboard.

OPTIONAL SKILL 7—ESOPHAGEAL TRACHEAL COMBITUBE

Before beginning, review pages 51–52 in your instructor's guide.

Minimum instructors needed: 1

Objectives

Upon completion of this skill station, the student should be able to

1. Explain the five essential points about use of this airway.
2. Correctly insert the Combitube®.

Equipment List

Item	Quantity
Adult intubation mannequins	2
Combitube airways	2
Cans of silicone lubricant spray	2
35-cc syringes	2
Tonsil suctions tip (Yaunker) and suction tubing	2
Bag-valve devices	2
Nonsterile rubber gloves	1 box
Face shields or goggles	2

Introduced in the early 1970s, blind-insertion airway devices (BIADs) were designed for use by EMS personnel who were not trained to intubate the trachea. All of these devices (EOA, EGTA, PtL, and Combitube) are designed to be inserted into the pharynx without the need for a laryngoscope to visualize where the tube is going. All of these devices have a tube with an inflatable cuff that is designed to seal the esophagus, thus preventing vomiting and aspiration of stomach contents as well as preventing gastric distention during bag-valve-mask or demand-valve-mask ventilation. It was also thought that by sealing the esophagus more air would enter the lungs and ventilation would be improved. These devices have their own dangers and require careful evaluation to be sure that they are in the correct position. None of the BIADs are equal to the endotracheal tube, which has become the invasive airway of choice for advanced EMS providers.

The Combitube is like the PtL airway in that it has a double lumen. However, in the Combitube, the two lumens are separated by a partition rather than one being inside of the other. One tube is sealed at the distal end and there are perforations in the area of the tube that would be in the pharynx. When the long tube is in the esophagus, the patient is ventilated through this short tube. The long tube is open at the distal end and it has a cuff that is blown up to seal the esophagus or the trachea, depending on which it has entered. When inserted, if the long tube goes into the esophagus, the cuff is inflated and the patient is ventilated through the short tube. If the long tube goes into the trachea, the cuff is inflated and the patient is ventilated through the long tube. Like the PtL airway, this device has a pharyngeal balloon that seals the pharynx and prevents blood and mucus from entering the airway from above. The Combitube is somewhat quicker and easier to insert than the PtL airway but, as with the other BIADs, you must be sure that you are ventilating the lungs and not the stomach.

You must remember five essential points about the Combitube:

1. Use only in patients who are unresponsive and without protective reflexes.

2. Do not use in any patient with an injury to the esophagus (e.g., caustic ingestions) or in children who are under the age of 15 and of average height and weight.

3. Pay careful attention to proper placement. Unrecognized intratracheal placement of the long tube is a lethal complication that produces complete airway obstruction. Such an occurrence is not always easy to detect, and the results are catastrophic. Like the EGTA and PtL, one of the great disadvantages of this airway is the fact that you can determine correct placement only by auscultation and observation of chest movement. Both may be quite unreliable in the prehospital setting.

4. You must insert gently and without force.

5. If the patient regains consciousness, you must remove the Combitube as it will cause retching and vomiting.

Procedure

1. Insert the tube blindly, watching for the two black rings on the Combitube that are used for measuring the depth of insertion. These rings should be positioned between the teeth and the lips.

2. Use the large syringe to inflate the pharyngeal cuff with 100 cc of air. When inflated, the Combitube will seat itself in the posterior pharynx behind the hard palate.

3. Use the small syringe to fill the distal cuff with 10–15 cc of air.

4. The long tube will usually go into the esophagus. Ventilate through the esophageal connector. It is the external tube that is the longer of the two and is marked #1. As with the PtL airway, you must see the chest rise, hear breath sounds, feel good compliance, and hear no breath sounds over the epigastrium in order to be sure that the long tube is in the esophagus.

5. If you do not see the chest rise, hear breath sounds, feel good compliance, and you hear breath sounds over the epigastrium, the tube has been placed in the trachea. In this case, change the ventilator to the shorter tracheal connector, which is marked #2. Again you must check to see the chest rise, hear breath sounds, feel good compliance, and hear no breath sounds over the epigastrium in order to be sure that you are ventilating the lungs.

Like the EGTA and PtL, if the patient becomes conscious, you must remove the Combitube. Extubation is likely to cause vomiting; be prepared to suction the pharynx and turn the backboard.

OPTIONAL SKILL 8—LARYNGEAL MASK AIRWAY

Before beginning, review pages 51–52 in your instructor's guide.

Minimum instructors needed: 1

Objectives

Upon completion of this skill station the student, should be able to

1. Explain the five essential points about use of the airway.
2. Correctly insert the Laryngeal Mask Airway (LMA®).

Important Points

The laryngeal mask airway (LMA) was developed for use as an alternative to the face mask for achieving and maintaining control of the airway during routine anesthetic procedures in the operating room. Since it does not protect the airway against vomiting and aspiration it was meant to be used in patients who had been fasting and thus had an empty stomach. It was later found to be useful in the emergency situation when intubation is not possible and you can't ventilate with a BVM. It may prevent having to do a surgical procedure to open the airway. The LMA is another blind-insertion airway device (BIAD) but differs from the others in that it was never designed to seal the esophagus and was not originally meant for emergency use. It is not equal to the endotracheal tube and should only be used when efforts to intubate the trachea have been unsuccessful and ventilation is compromised.

You must remember these essential points about the LMA:

1. Use only for patients who are unresponsive and without protective reflexes. If the patient still has a gag reflex the LMA may cause laryngospasm or vomiting.
2. Do not use for any patient with an injury to the esophagus (e.g., caustic ingestions) or in children who are less than 30 kg.
3. Lubricate only the posterior surface of the LMA to avoid blockage of the aperture or aspiration of the lubricant.
4. Patients should be adequately monitored (constant visual monitoring, cardiac monitor, and if possible, pulse oximeter) at all times during LMA use.
5. To avoid trauma to the airway, force should never be used during LMA insertion.
6. Never overinflate the cuff after insertion. Overinflation may cause malposition, loss of seal, or trauma. Cuff pressure should be checked periodically.
7. If airway problems persist or ventilation is inadequate, the LMA should be removed and reinserted or an airway established by other means.
8. The LMA does not prevent aspiration if the patient vomits. The presence of a nasogastric tube does not rule out the possibility of regurgitation and may even make regurgitation more likely because the tube makes the esophageal sphincter incompetent.
9. If the patient regains consciousness, you must remove the LMA as it will cause retching and vomiting.

Procedure

1. Ventilate with mouth-to-mask or bag-valve mask and suction the pharynx prior to insertion of the airway.

2. Remove the valve tab and check the integrity of the LMA cuff by inflating with the maximum volume of air (see Table 9–1 below).

3. The cuff of the LMA should be tightly *deflated* using the enclosed syringe so that it forms a flat oval disk with the rim facing away from the aperture. This can be accomplished by pressing the mask with its hollow side down on a sterile flat surface. Use the fingers to guide the cuff into an oval. Shape and attempt to eliminate any wrinkles on the distal edge of the cuff. A completely flat and smooth leading edge facilitates insertion, avoids contact with the epiglottis, and is important to assure success when positioning the device.

4. Lubricate the posterior surface of the LMA with a water-soluble lubricant just before insertion.

5. Preoxygenate the patient.

6. If there is no danger of spinal injury, position the patient with the neck flexed and the head extended. If the mechanism of injury suggests the potential for spinal injury, the head and neck must be maintained in a neutral position.

7. Hold the LMA like a pen, with the index finger placed at the junction of the cuff and the tube. Under direct vision, press the tip of the cuff upward against the hard palate and flatten the cuff against it. The black line on the airway tube should be oriented anteriorly toward the upper lip.

8. Use the index finger to guide the LMA, pressing upward and backward toward the ears in one smooth movement. Advance the LMA into the hypopharynx until a definite resistance is felt.

9. Before removing the index finger, gently press down on the tube with the other hand to prevent the LMA from being pulled out of place.

10. Without holding the tube, inflate the cuff with just enough air to obtain a seal. The maximum volumes are shown in Table 9–1.

11. Connect the LMA to the BVM and employ manual ventilation of less than 20 cm H_2O (this precludes use of a FROPVD unless you use one that allows you to set the pressure). As with the BIADs, you must see the chest rise, hear breath sounds, feel good compliance, and hear no breath sounds over the epigastrium in order to be sure that the LMA is correctly placed.

12. Insert a bite block (not an oropharyngeal airway) and secure the LMA with tape. Remember that the LMA does not protect the airway from aspiration. If the patient becomes conscious, the LMA must be removed. Extubation is likely to cause vomiting; be prepared to suction the pharynx and turn the backboard.

TABLE 9–1.

LMA Size	Patient Size	Maximum Cuff Volumes (air only)
3	Children >30 kg and small adults	20 mL
2	Normal and large adults	30 mL
1	Large adults	40 mL

Note: Never overinflate the cuff. Avoid prolonged intracuff pressures greater than 60 cm H_2O.

OPTIONAL SKILL 9—ADULT INTRAOSSEOUS INFUSION

Before beginning, review pages 51–52 in your instructor's guide.

Minimum instructors needed: 1

Objectives

Upon completion of this skill station, the student should be able to

1. Explain the indications for the use of adult intraosseous infusion.
2. Perform an adult intraosseous infusion.

Standard vascular access in the adult patient involves the peripheral venous system. Under conditions common in trauma, the peripheral veins often collapse. Intraosseous infusion (IO) for the pediatric patient has been taught within the BTLS course and has been common practice for several years. In the past, adult IO was used in some cases to give medications, but the flow rate was too slow for it to be used for fluid resuscitation of adult trauma patients. Recently, a device (F.A.S.T. 1®) has been developed which allows rapid fluid replacement and allows adult IO to be used for fluid resuscitation as well as administration of medications. This device makes use of the sternum for the site because

1. The sternal body is large, relatively flat, and can be readily located.
2. The sternum retains a high proportion of red marrow.
3. The F.A.S.T. 1 device has a thinner, more uniform cortical bone covering overlying a relatively uniform marrow space.
4. It is less likely to be fractured than the extremities, particularly at the level of the manubrium.
5. It is usually exposed, or easy to expose, in a trauma patient.
6. The recommended infusion site on the midline of the manubrium, 15 mm below the sternal notch, is easy to locate and landmark.
7. There is not an appreciable time lag between central venous infusion and IO infusion of most substances. For adult trauma patients who need fluid resuscitation or medications and you are unable to quickly obtain a peripheral IV line, this device may be the vascular access of choice. It is fast (60–90 seconds), simple (failure rate <5%), safe (the device positions the infusion tube at a controlled depth), and has adequate flow rates (30 mL/min by gravity, 125 mL/min by pressure-cuffed IV bag, and 250 mL/min by syringe).

Indications

1. The adult patient who is in cardiac arrest and in whom you cannot quickly obtain peripheral venous access
2. Hypovolemic adult patients who have a prolonged transport and in whom you are unable to quickly (two sticks or 90 seconds) obtain peripheral venous access

Contraindications

1. Do not use this device if the sternum is fractured.
2. Recent sternotomy (may have compromised the integrity of the manubrium or its vascularization).
3. Severe osteoporosis or bone softening conditions.

Important Points on Adult Intraosseous Infusion

1. As with all advanced procedures, this technique must be accepted local protocol, and you must obtain medical direction (protocol or verbal) before performing.

2. If infiltration occurs (rare), you must abort the procedure. This is the only bone in which this device is used.

3. Potential complications are
   a. Subperiostial infusion due to improper placement
   b. Osteomyelitis
   c. Sepsis
   d. Fat embolism
   e. Marrow damage

Studies have shown these complications to be rare; however, good aseptic technique is important, just as with intravenous therapy.

Procedure

1. Place the Target Patch at the site. The single recommended site of insertion is the adult manubrium, on the midline and 1.5 cm (5/8") below the sternal notch. The site is prepped with aseptic technique, and the index finger is used to align the Target Patch with the patient's sternal notch.

2. With the Patch securely attached to the patient's skin, the Introducer is placed in the target zone, perpendicular to the skin. A firm push on the Introducer releases the Infusion Tube into the correct site and to the right penetration depth. The Introducer is pulled straight back, exposing the Infusion Tube and a two-part support sleeve, which falls away.

3. Correct placement is verified by observation of marrow entering the Infusion Tube. The Infusion Tube is joined to tubing on the patch, which is connected to a purged source of fluid. Fluid can now flow to the patient.

4. The Protector Dome is pressed down firmly over the Target Patch to engage the Velcro fastening. The site is clearly visible through the Dome, the Infusion Tube and connection tubing move easily without any strain on the skin, and the site requires no further stabilization while the patient is transported.

FORMS

The following forms are available from BTLS International and can be obtained as a packet by calling 1-800-495-BTLS (outside the U.S.: 630-495-6442).

Course Coordinator Worksheet
Course Budget
Course Request Form
Postcourse Checklist
Model Selection Form
Course Roster (Mandatory for reporting)
Course Roster Tally Sheet (Mandatory for reporting)
Sample Letter to Course Instructors

Sample Letter to Course Registrants
Affiliate Faculty Course Evaluation
Provider Course Application Form
Instructor Course Application Form
Instructor Reciprocity Form
Instructor Recertification Form
Course Lecture Evaluation
Practical Skills Evaluation
Practical Station Evaluation
Practical Testing Evaluation

GLASGOW COMA SCORE

Eye Opening	Points	Verbal Response	Points	Motor Response	Points
Spontaneous	4	Oriented	5	Obeys commands	6
To voice	3	Confused	4	Localizes pain	5
To pain	2	Inappropriate words	3	Withdraws	4
None	1	Incomprehensible sounds	2	Abnormal flexion	3*
		Silent	1	Abnormal extension	2**
				No movement	1

*Decorticate posturing to pain
**Decerebrate posturing to pain

NOTES

NOTES

NOTES

NOTES

NOTES